Little Book of
Love Magic

Patricia Telesco

THE CROSSING PRESS
FREEDOM, CALIFORNIA

Copyright © 1999 by Patricia Telesco
Cover design by Victoria May
Cover illustration by Teresa Mallen
Interior design by Karen Narita
Printed in the U.S.A.
3rd Printing, 2000

For information on bulk purchases or group discounts for this and other Crossing Press titles, please contact our Special Sales Manager at 800/777-1048.
Visit our Web site: www.crossingpress.com

Library of Congress Cataloging-in-Publication Data

Telesco, Patricia, 1960-
    A little book of love magic / Patricia Telesco.
        p. cm.
    Includes bibliographical references.
    ISBN 0-89594-887-7
    1. Magic. 2. Love--Miscellanea. I. Title.
BF1623.L6T45   1999
133.4'42--dc21   98-49315
                                                            CIP

Contents

Preface

If you find the idea of casting spells and making charms daunting, put your mind at ease. The methods in this book require very little other than willpower, commitment, and patience.

Willpower directs the process of personal transformation, which begins in your mind and soul. This means trusting yourself and believing in your spiritual nature as a force for positive change. When you have this force in yourself and your judgment, love magic will flow more easily and intuitively.

Sometimes the universe tests our determination. When difficulties arise, commitment will support both you and your magic. So, pledge yourself to love's quest until you succeed, then commit to maintaining that energy in a relationship. Finally, patience makes the waiting game a little easier to bear. Magic isn't a quick fix for all of love's difficulties—but it will help you clear the path so there are fewer bumps along the way.

If you plan to use this book to attract potential lovers, a word to the wise before you begin: Love magic does not function well if you're using it out of fear of being alone. Fear leads to hasty action which usually fails. Nature and the universe have their own sense of timing that must be accepted and respected for magic to work for the greatest good in your life and the lives of those with whom you're involved.

Above all, keep your expectations in balance, using magical energy to create opportunities that correspond to your needs. Once magic opens love's door, you can choose to step through or not. Take your time and trust your heart to know which opportunities can lead to long-term happiness.

Introduction

"Fall in love over and over again every day. Love your family, your neighbors, your enemies, and yourself. And don't stop with humans. Love animals, plants, stones, even galaxies."
——Frederic and Mary Ann Brussat, *Spiritual Literacy*

Love makes the world go round. It plays with our fancy, provokes daydreams, confuses us with its complexities, and propels us in everything we do from making war to artistic masterpieces.

People throughout time have been "in love" with love. No matter the era or setting, the quest for a mate, the need to be cherished, and the hope that love will remain strong have all been perennial themes in literature, music, and art. Love is at the very heart of what it is to be human. As long as there are writers, musicians, and artists, love will remain a best-seller.

Village elders, shamans, and religious leaders also attended to matters of the heart, using the more direct approach that this book emulates. A priest or priestess blesses unions with divine authority. Elders listen to couples' troubles with a non-judgmental ear. Shamans turn to the spirits of nature and the energy of magic to help people find love, assure devotion, and keep passion alive.

While the relationship game has changed much over time, our need for love has not. No matter where you look in our society, you find the spirit of love and romance. A song on the radio tells the story of a relationship. A billboard portrays two lovers gazing at each other. A movie features a midnight rendezvous or an afternoon tryst. Over and over, the spirit of love finds expression in our day-to-day lives.

This book helps you use magic as a force for manifesting your hopes and dreams. When I use the word "love," however, I am not talking only about romantic relationships. Love has a far greater scope than that. It includes friendships, feelings towards pets, spiritual love, and love or passion for our work.

When you want to increase your personal magnetism, when you need a spell to ease heartache, a charm to enrich friendship, a talisman to improve self-esteem, a potion for romance, or a ritual to deepen commitment, turn to this guide and start making magic! Taking this kind of initiative will restore your confidence and inspire hope. A person's self-confidence and hope work powerful magic all by themselves. From there, it is a short step to igniting the mystical fires of love and keeping them burning, every moment of every day.

CHAPTER I

Love Harbingers, Superstitions, and Divinations

"Everyone carries with them at least one, and probably many pieces to someone else's puzzle. Sometimes they know it. Sometimes they don't."
—Lawrence Kushner, *Honey from the Rock*

No matter how futile it seems, human beings throughout history have used every available means to secure true love. Three of the most popular methods have also been the easiest: interpreting portents from nature and happenstance occurrences; following superstitious guidelines; and fortune-telling. This chapter explores these techniques and provides guidelines for trying them yourself.

FOLKLORE AND SIGNS

Outwardly, some of the omens, signs, and superstitions used in the past for seeking love, discerning potential lovers, and gauging love's depth may seem silly. Before judging our ancestors too harshly, however, remember that not too long ago, unmarried individuals were regarded as pitiful oddities, as evidenced in the pitiful way spinsters were whispered about with nods and winks. Consequently, young people found themselves anxious about their marital future. Folk cultures answered this apprehension with simple divinatory practices for aspiring lovers. By using similar methods we too can relieve our concerns about relationships now and in the future.

Catch Me if You Can

Before you can fall in love, you have to find the right person. But how do you know that Mr. or Ms. *Right* isn't just another Mr. or Ms. *Wrong?* Arabian lore tells us that spying a hoopoe bird means that someone is thinking fondly of you. Victorian tradition says that seeing two doves fighting means you and your present mate are ill-suited. On the other hand, if you see a bluebird, happiness in a relationship is on the horizon.

Should you decide to venture out into the singles scene, peel an apple in an unbroken coil before you go. Twirl the peel in the air three times, then toss it over your left shoulder and see what letter it resembles when it lands. This reveals an initial in the name of a potential lover. Eat the fruit for healthy self-love, and toss the seeds into a fire. If they pop and fly, your soon-to-be lover will be true and passionate. Alternatively, press a seed on each cheek. If the left one falls off first, your next relationship will prove unsound. If the right one falls first, expect a kiss. You can use the dried apple peel and seeds as effective symbolic components in your love spells and charms.

You can also observe omens and signs at mealtime. For example, receiving the last bit of food or drink at a meal means that your future mate will be good-looking. Receiving buttered bread and cake on the same plate portends a marriage proposal. When dessert comes around, check the surface of your pudding. If it's smooth and free of cracks, the forthcoming relationship will also run smoothly.

The Dating Game

Once you start seeing someone regularly, there are a few "dos" and "don'ts" recommended in old wives' tales. For example, never start dating steadily on a Friday, an unlucky day according to superstition. On the other hand, do put a silver coin in your shoe when going out on a date. This token encourages an engagement proposal.

Never hand anything sharp to your partner. This "cuts off" love. Similarly, never poke or stir your partner's fireplace, salt their food, sit on a table next to them, put shoes on their table, or give them shoes as a present. These actions stir up troubles and quarrels. Should you have an argument, finding a four-holed button shortly thereafter indicates better times are just around the corner. Keep this button with you as an amulet to protect from further negativity.

Loves Me, Loves Me Not

I have fond preteen memories of plucking daisy petals while saying "loves me, loves me not." It seemed to take forever to get around the blossom and find out if a relationship would work. The daisy remains a symbol of love, and plays a role in many kinds of love magic. Our ancestors also provided us with other signs to help us discern if the answer is, indeed, "loves me." Like the daisy, many of these signs or symbols can become effective components in love magic.

Watch the gifts that your present steady gives you. French tradition maintains that a lover who presents a bundle of honeysuckle flowers offers a harmonious relationship with the bouquet. Honeysuckle incense or oil is a good component for spells focused on harmony. Receiving a knot ring or pin from a suitor represents oneness and safety in that relationship. (We still call getting married "tying the knot.") Should you get a letter from your sweetheart written in red ink, however, beware. Bad luck in love and potential arguments lie in store for you.

While you and your lover walk together, carefully observe nature. If a willow leaf falls near your path, Chinese superstition says that the relationship is true and blessed by the gods. Wax and keep the leaf to preserve your love. If you spy three magpies flying together, you will soon marry.

Other sure signs of a forthcoming engagement include finding ring patterns in the hearth's ashes on New Year's Day, finding two loaves of bread joined together after baking, seeing a ring in a candle's flame, breaking open a two-yolked egg, finding a pin from a wedding dress, finding a bean in its shell in soup or stew, and passing a bride on her way up the stairs. Any of the items you find on this list can also be used in spells or act as tokens to empower your love magic.

To find out how long it will take for a marriage to follow an engagement, blow on a dandelion seed head or look at a horseshoe you have around for luck. The number of seeds remaining on the dandelion or holes in a horseshoe equals the number of years before taking your marriage vows. If you want to be **sure** you marry within a year, make pudding on Christmas and stir it clockwise. Whisper your wish into the pudding, then eat it to internalize its sweetness and to get lucky in love.

Love on the Mind

Wondering if that special someone is thinking fondly of you? According to Victorian belief, if your apron fell off, your sweetheart was reflecting on your relationship. For a married person, however, this was a sign that the marriage will soon face troubles. If your ears are ringing or your slip is falling, your special someone is thinking loving thoughts.

Marital Musts

The folklore of relationships is full of superstitions and signs surrounding marriage. Every action, from the way the couple bathed and dressed to the way they departed for the honeymoon could affect their future happiness and luck. Many brides still try to include something old, something new, something borrowed, and something blue in their wardrobe. This action weaves the past, present, and future together with pure intentions.

Other cultures have their traditions as well. In India, brides rinse their hands in henna on the morning of the wedding for good fortune. Other brides step over running water to make sure all bad luck is washed away. Many cultures feel that it is bad luck for a bride to see her life partner before the ceremony, or glimpse her reflection in the mirror after she's dressed. Seeing a cat before the ceremony and feeding it, however, brings good luck and beautiful weather. Wearing a bridal veil protects the bride from the evil eye, but a bride should never wear pearls, as they bring tears.

Among Hindus, carrying jasmine in the bridal bouquet ensures a happy marriage, and wearing bright clothing symbolizes devotion and joy. Specifically, a red sari bedecked with flower garlands reflects fidelity and happiness.

As the bridal party enters the church, each member must step on the right foot first to get the relationship off on the "right foot." Around the sacred space, a few bouquets should house blue knotted ribbons to ensure the couple's devotion and constancy. If the sun shines during the ceremony, it indicates divine blessing and good luck.

Exchanging gold rings ensures eternal unity. At the end of a wedding ceremony, binding the couple's hands with a cloth tied in three knots brings divine sanctification of the marriage and the couple's unity. In China, the couple kneels before ancestral tablets to honor their social unit and ensure their ancestor's blessings.

As newlyweds leave the church, showering them with rice, flower petals, or confetti brings fertility, passion, and abundance. This tradition has had global appeal, appearing in ceremonies in the West and in the East.

Romans began the custom of the couple eating the wedding cake together, thus bringing harmony to the couple and their family. If the cake looks and tastes good, the marriage will likewise turn out well. Silver bells on a wedding cake have been said to keep away evil spirits. At least one piece of this cake should be preserved for the couple's first wedding anniversary to continue their happiness.

In some countries, including Macedonia, Norway, and the Ukraine, coins are baked into the cake to ensure the couple's future providence and prosperity. A piece of this cake is eaten on each day of the honeymoon. As the couple leaves for their honeymoon, shoes tied on the car ensure that the two will always be followed by luck.

Devotion and Fidelity

Is your lover unfaithful? Our ancestors had this problem too! One remedy was to keep the hearth fire of the home always burning, to safeguard the ongoing love and commitment in the home.

If you receive a gift that includes a starfish, in Europe this means eternal, unwavering love. The gift of a swan feather symbolizes fidelity and devotion, and if you accept a sprig of fresh yarrow, you will be bound to the giver for seven years of constant love. Using this symbolism add a starfish, feather, or leaf to an attraction charm.

You should never stir your lover's drink. If you do, he will be unfaithful. On the other hand, you should always kiss your love good-bye in the morning. He or she will live longer and your devotion to each other will grow. If you aren't meeting your sweetheart regularly, drink wine in which rose and vervain have been steeped. It will encourage a kiss and increased fidelity, especially if you drank it at midnight on Midsummer's Eve (June 24).

LOVE IS IN THE MOON

The moon is used in all types of magic. The waxing moon represents growth, the full moon fulfillment, fertility and maturity, and the waning moon closure. Esoteric traditions link the moon with the feminine intuitive. This, combined with the romantic associations of moonlight, make the moon the perfect agent for spells and predictions about love.

For example, a first date under a waxing to full moon gives the relationship a better chance of being happy than one begun under a waning moon. According to ancient traditions, crescent moons increase personal beauty and endow the person with enough energy to maintain a healthy relationship. The full moon of May improves the fertility of a relationship and empowers relationship spells; the June full moon empowers all types of relationship magic; and the full Hunter's Moon of October aids the search for a life mate.

You can combine these lunar events with oracular efforts for the greatest effect. For example, to know when you will meet someone special, or get married, hold a silk square over a body of water with the full moon of October behind you. The number of reflections seen through the scarf indicates the number of months you must wait. This is a type of scrying, from an old English tradition.

When you do meet a potential mate, pay attention to the moon sign. It will predict the course of that relationship, and the most positive actions you can take with that person. This particular form of sign and omen interpretation is a part of astrology that can also be utilized effectively in timing love spells and any divinatory efforts:

> *Moon in Aries*—Take a chance! An Aries moon enhances spells that help you make a choice. You can divine the answers to questions that will influence your decision.

> *Moon in Taurus*—Be cautious. This is a bad time for drastic changes. A Taurus moon enhances spells that deepen devotion. Divine the answers to questions that focus on a relationship's emotional, monetary, or spiritual security.

> *Moon in Gemini*—Accentuate playfulness and communication. A Gemini moon enhances spells to rein in a fickle lover. Divine the answers to questions that focus on a mate's fidelity and trustworthiness.

Moon in Cancer—Keep emotions in balance. A Cancer moon enhances spells to increase understanding. Divine the answers to questions where you need improved insight and perspective.

Moon in Leo—Socialize and make a good impression. A propitious time for a relationship to start. A Leo moon enhances spells designed for glamoury. Divine the answers to questions that determine if a certain person is interested or elsewhere committed.

Moon in Virgo—Make an intellectual connection. A Virgo moon enhances spells designed to encourage a healthy relationship. Divine the answers to questions about when and where a good relationship will begin, or if a present relationship will improve.

Moon in Libra—Emphasize friendship and mutual creative interests. A Libra moon enhances spells designed to improve personal charm. Divine the answers to questions of friendship.

Moon in Scorpio—Focus on family, but avoid arguments. A Scorpio moon enhances spells designed to augment sensitivity between people. Divine the answers to questions about the home, domesticity, or matters of communication.

Moon in Sagittarius—Be honest and thoughtful; break out of outmoded routines. A Sagittarius moon enhances spells designed for the adventurous spirit. Divine the answers to questions in which you need to hear the whole truth.

Moon in Capricorn—Be practical and tenacious. A Capricorn moon enhances spells designed to increase self-discipline. Divine the answers to questions focused on obstacles that impede a relationship.

Moon in Aquarius—Socialize and listen to new ideas. An Aquarius moon enhances spells designed to smooth love's pathway. Divine the answers to questions that provide wisdom and guidance on the next steps to take.

Moon in Pisces—Seek advice and trust your instincts. A Pisces moon enhances spells designed to cultivate spiritual love. Divine the answers to questions that will improve your decision making before you consider a leap of faith.

FORTUNE-TELLING

If waiting patiently for omens or doing rituals isn't your cup of tea, try divining the present and future. For every passively observed sign, portent, and bit of folk wisdom, there is at least one active divination method available. The fortune-telling techniques presented here are easy to perform in a variety of settings. The objects and ingredients are all easily found in nature or your own home.

Dreaming of Love

In order to frame your dreams about present or future loves, a pillow stuffed with mugwort, rose, mint, and lemon verbena can help. Or make tea from these herbs (1/2 teaspoon each dried herb to a cup of water). Drink the tea before bed. On St. Thomas' Eve, have an onion with your tea; on St. Agnes' Day, eat a salted egg. Both foods further increase your chances of incubating an insightful or prophetic dream.

Or try putting an ivy leaf under your pillow on New Year's Day, vervain and yarrow under your pillow on St. Agnes' Eve. On Valentine's Day put two bay leaves sprinkled with rose water under your pillow. All these actions evoke prophetic dreams. Putting a piece of wedding cake under your pillow, or nine leaves of any kind tied into a cloth with nine knots, will have similar results on any night of the year.

Place a prayer book, a key, a ring, a flower, a piece of willow, a piece of bread, or cards under your pillow. Whichever item you dream of indicates the state of your love life: the book represents a forthcoming marriage; the key, an opportunity to meet someone special; the flower, blossoming relationship; the willow, a need for flexibility; the bread, a secure relationship; and the cards, a risky relationship.

To know who your future lover will be, look at the new moon over your right shoulder and say, *New Moon, tell me please, who my love is fated to be.* Go to bed without speaking another word and dreams of the future will come to you. Or you can wait for the first new moon of a new year and repeat the following incantation three times while looking at the moon, *New Moon, let me see, who my love shall finally be.* You will have prophetic dreams that night (see also "Love is in the Moon," earlier in this chapter).

Other symbols that appear in dreams may be directly related to current or future relationships. While not every dream will contain symbolic content about your love life, if this subject lies heavy on your mind, the chance of insights appearing in a dream will increase.

Ancient and modern dream keys contain literally hundreds of images and interpretations specific to love in all its forms. Some examples follow here. As you read them, please bear in mind that dream interpretation is an imperfect art. You are unique, and what your dreams mean to you is specific to you. Use this list to spur more personalized insights. And remember to write your dreams in a notebook or record them on tape so you can reflect upon them later.

Love's Dream Keys

Acorn, shaking from a tree—a successful relationship
Air, cold—a similarly cold domestic relationship
Alabaster—a forthcoming marriage

Amethyst, losing—a failed affair or engagement

Anchor—an argument with a sweetheart

Angels—a disturbing influence in a relationship or
    a scandal in love

Aroma, sweet—a pleasant surprise in a relationship

Ax—a worthy, but not wealthy lover

Bachelor—a bad time to enter into a new relationship

Banana—an uninteresting or unexciting mate

Bet—an engagement offer that may not be a good choice

Bird, caged—a wealthy marriage

Bird, speaking—an opportunity to improve communications
    between yourself and another

Bolt—an obstacle to a relationship

Bride, kissing—a reconciliation

Burr—a possessive lover or tangled relationships

Butterfly—a forthcoming happy union

Cabbage—an unfaithful companion

Camping—a lover who has trouble with commitment

Candles, making—an unexpected proposal

Car, riding in—a relationship impeded by jealousy
    or rivalry

Carrot—a child or a more fruitful relationship

Caterpillar—a hypocritical companion causing a loss in love

Celery, eating—a boundless love coming to you

Champion—a developing warm friendship

Charity—a deceitful rival

Chestnut, eating—a well-to-do lover coming your way
Child, beautiful—a happy union and reciprocal love
Chrysanthemum—an engagement
Cider, drinking—an unfaithful friend
Clothing, black—a disagreement or quarrel
Clothing, blue—a supportive and loyal friend
Clothing, rejecting out-of-date—a new relationship
    or renewed love
Clouds, transparent—a relationship's troubles clearing up
Coffee, drinking—a quarrel and disapproving attitudes
    between you and someone close
Coin, receiving from lover—a rejection
Coral, white—an unfaithful lover
Cows, milking—a hope or desire fulfilled
Cucumber—a pleasant change in a relationship
Deer—a pure, deep friendship
Dentist—a reason to doubt a companion's sincerity
Dishes, stacked—a successful marriage
Dog bite—a forthcoming quarrel
Ducks, flying—a new home and potential for marriage
Eel—the end of a long, difficult courtship
Embrace, lovers—a quarrel caused by infidelity
Eye—appearance of a rival in love
Fables, telling—a new romantic interest or attachment
Face, sweetheart's—an unexpected breakup in a previously
    happy relationship

Fair—a jovial, even-tempered companion coming into your life

Fawn—a faithful lover

Fear—a reason to doubt a relationship

Fighting—slander and gossip caused by an unworthy companion

Fish—a good-looking, sexually delightful lover

Flute, playing—a lover with charm and charisma

Fork—an unhappy domestic partnership

Garbage—a friend or lover who deserts you

Gate, broken—a disharmonious association

Gold, gift of—a wealthy associate

Guitar, hearing—a flattering, persuasive friend who tempts you

Gypsy telling fortunes—a hasty commitment that's filled with jealousy

Hail—end of a long time alone; a happy love affair

Hair, tangled—a troublesome or burdensome relationship

Heartache—a lazy lover who causes distress

Hen—a pleasant reunion with a friend or lover

Honey, eating—a commitment bringing love, passion, and joy

Ice, floating—disruption caused by a jealous, ill-tempered friend

Ink, spilling—a relationship experiencing trouble due to slander and envy

Ivy, clinging—a happy rendezvous

Jail, lover in—a disappointing character; deceit

Jelly—a pleasant reunion with a friend

Jumping down a well—a reckless decision in love

Keys, broken—a separation caused by jealousy

Keys, unlocking with—a companion in whom you place too much confidence

Kiss, lover—a harmonious relationship

Kiss, blowing—a separation from loved ones

Knife, broken—a defeat in love

Knot, tied—a nagging lover or friend

Labyrinth—an entanglement

Lace—a devoted, faithful lover

Leather—a favorable meeting or engagement

Legs, admiring—a charming person who causes you to act silly

Lemon, shriveled—a separation

Lips, swollen—an unhealthy romantic desire

Marriage, attending—a thoughtful loved one

Mice—a problem at home due to uncertainty

Mirror, looking in—a breakup that brings disappointment

Moons, two—a difficult choice that may lead to losing a lover

Mud, walking in—a family disturbance

Needle, finding—help from an appreciative friend

Nuts, gathering—a favor from a lover

Oak—a long-term relationship that offers stability

Ocean, calm—a charming companion to spend time with

Olives, breaking a bottle of—an impotent, disappointing
   sexual encounter
Parsley, eating—a large family
Peaches, gathering—a worldly-wise, wealthy lover
Pebbles, walking in—appearance of a selfish rival
Photo album, looking at—a new lover who will be good for you
Pine—a successful, strong relationship
Priest/Priestess—a true friend
Quicksand—a deception or dangerous liaison
Rabbit, white—a faithful, devoted lover
Rain seen through a window—a passionate, requited love
Rice, eating—a comfortable domestic life
Ropes—a physical encounter plagued with uncertainty
Salve—an enemy becoming a friend
Scissors, breaking—a quarrel
Shark, dead—a reconciliation
Smoke—a relationship clouded with doubt and fear
Spider web—a secure relationship and good home
Stomach, shrunken—false friends or a forthcoming betrayal
Table, empty—a disagreement leading to disappointment
Tea, borrowing—an indiscretion
Tent, torn—a troublesome person revealed
Thorns—a dissatisfaction with a relationship or barriers to
   be overcome
Topaz, receiving—an interesting affair
Umbrella, borrowing—a misunderstanding between friends
Valentine, receiving—an ardent lover

Veil, wearing—a partner's insincerity

Violets—a meeting with a potential long-term mate

Wall, jumping over—overcoming an obstacle to a relationship through perseverance

Water sports—a loving, passionate encounter

Wedding ring, shiny—a sincere relationship

Windows, closed—a friend or lover who deserts you

Wolf—a betrayal

Zoo—a love affair that has varied luck

Love's Fires

Fire symbolizes love and passion. Consequently, the ancient art of pyromancy is a good vehicle for love divination. Begin with a fire made from either cedar, juniper, or sandalwood chips. When you ignite the fire, watch to see what happens. The behavior of the flames indicates your answer as follows:

Blue flames—a relationship that undergoes spiritual or emotional storms

Bright flames—a relationship filled with healthy passion

Burning with two points—a balanced relationship in which both parties are independent

Burning with three points—a relationship vexed by a rival or external interests, or one that requires the help of friends to get started

Catching fire after a delay—a relationship that requires some nurturing and diligence to be successful

Clear, even flames—a pure, even-tempered relationship

Heart-shaped flame—a relationship filled with mutual love
Not catching fire—a lack of interest or passion
One-sided fire—a relationship that is imbalanced
Pale flames—a relationship that may prove unhealthy
Ring-shaped fire—a relationship that leads to marriage
Rising up, then fading quickly—a relationship that begins with intense passion but burns itself out
Slow-burning—a relationship where taking your time results in long-term devotion
Smoke without any fire—a relationship filled with illusions, falsehood, and insecurity
Smoldering with lots of smoke—a relationship in which one partner puts on facades, causing strife
Sparks—a relationship with all the right kindling, but which may undergo some problems from hot tempers
Spitting or roaring—a relationship filled with arguments as well as fiery passion

If you don't have the suggested woods available, toss an herb, flower, or some incense on the fire instead. Choose the plant or incense according to your question (see Appendix A) and observe. Interpret the flames from the herb or flower as above, and also interpret any images that form in the smoke similarly to dream key images. Observe the smoke's movements as follows:

Doesn't burn—a bad sign. This situation probably won't work, or will take a lot of effort to get moving in the right direction

Hovers around the flame—an ominous sign indicating a
  possessive lover or mate
Rises straight up—a good sign telling you to move ahead with
  confidence; knowing that the divine sees your needs
Rises to the right—a sign that love's path should be smooth
Rises to the left—a warning to proceed with caution, or stop
  and wait for better timing
Rises, then divides—a good start, but watch the road—
  it could be bumpy

Blossoming Relationships

Plants, especially flowers, can be used in many forms of love divination other than pyromancy. For example, plant two flowers
that symbolize you and your friend or loved one. By each, put a
piece of paper bearing your names in the soil. While you work,
focus intently on your question regarding the relationship. If the
flowers grow and twine together, this represents a good match
for a long-term commitment. If they grow equally, side-by-side,
it predicts a good friendship based on equality. If the flower
heads turn away from one another after blossoming, affections
are not mutual. Finally, if either flower grows ill or dies, this
means the relationship may have unhealthy tendencies.

You can also make herb or flower pendulums for divination.
Choose a flower or herb that relates to your question, such as
bay leaf to tell the strength of a relationship. Tie the plant at
the end of a length of thread. Hold the other end between

your thumb and forefinger over a designated spot, perhaps a piece of paper bearing your question or the name of your present partner. Put your elbow on the table, still the pendulum, and concentrate on your question. Give yourself some time; the pendulum may not move immediately. Interpret the movements as follows:

Circles, clockwise—a positive answer; harmony and joy

Circles, counterclockwise—a negative answer; difficulty

Diagonals—an ominous answer; problems that weigh heavily on your relationship, possibly causing depression

Ellipsis, east-west—a positive answer; strong, emotional love

Ellipsis, north-south—an indefinite answer; an intuitive relationship

Horizontal lines—a positive answer; physical and sexually pleasing mate

Up-down movement—a potentially negative answer indicating a divide to overcome

Vertical lines—a generally negative answer indicating a domineering mate, rival, or an overpowering situation

If you find this approach doesn't adequately answer your question, put out symbolic markers in a circle at twelve points corresponding to hours on a clock. Determine ahead of time what each marker represents with regard to your question. Put your elbow on the outside of these markers, and the pendulum point in the center. Then close your eyes and concentrate on your question. Keep your eyes closed until you feel the pendulum moving, then open your eyes to see which marker it is indicating. Some potential symbols could include:

Apple slice—a healthy relationship

Balloon—an inflated ego or a situation blown out of proportion

Crayon—an immature relationship

Die—a risky relationship that could be positive or negative

Eraser—a mistake that can be corrected

Eyeglasses—an uncertain situation; look closer before making a decision

Glue—a secure relationship, but possibly over-possessive

House—a new residence, or improved security

Knife or scissors—a breakup or severe argument

Light bulb—good advice offered by a trusted companion

Paper clip—a connection that could use improvement

Pencil or pen—a forthcoming communication from a friend or lover

Salt—a relationship preserved through wisdom

Tape—a problem to repair before it gets worse

Wheelbarrow—a relationship's progress slowed or stopped by emotional baggage

Tea Leaves and Coffee Clouds

Originating with the gypsies, this is simple and fun. Begin with a cup of tea made from loose tea leaves or herb parts. Think of your question while you enjoy the tea. When only a few drops of liquid remain, hold the cup in your left hand and swirl it three times clockwise. Overturn the cup, tap it lightly, then turn it right side up to see the images formed by any remaining tea leaves. Symbols closer to the rim reflect current situations, while those at the bottom reflect forthcoming situations. Use the following guide and the previous dream symbol list to interpret your tea leaves:

Love's Tea Leaf Key

Acorn—a successful affair or victory over a rival

Anchor—a home or new residence

Bat—a friend whose motivations should be questioned

Bell—a wedding or engagement announcement

Butterfly—a vain person, or a relationship undergoing drastic transformations

Cat—a fickle companion, or a relationship experiencing a fresh start

Clock—a situation where you need to act quickly

Clouds—a difficult situation which must get worse before it gets better

Clumps—a delay in finding love or working out a problem with an established relationship

Dice—a risk that can go either way

Dog—a faithful, devoted lover or friend

Ear—a relationship where one partner needs to listen more closely

Fire—a hasty action that may bring arguments

Glass—a fragile emotional situation

Hammer—a relationship filled with tension

Horse—a new or rekindled relationship in which you risk getting carried away

Initials—the name of a person that somehow affects the present situation, or who is intimately involved in this question's solution

Ivy—a faithful companion or a clingy relationship

Lock—a selfish relationship or a barrier to overcome

People—a new association

Question mark—a feeling of uncertainty that overshadows a relationship

Ring—a reliable friendship or engagement proposal

Snake—a change in sexual interest or energy

Tree—a wish for a fulfilling relationship

Umbrella—a stormy relationship where some protection is offered

Volcano—a very passionate relationship

Web—an entangling situation; watch your step

Wheel—patient, paced progress

If you're an ardent coffee drinker, this method can also work. Drink half a cup of black coffee while thinking about your question. Then slowly pour in some cream. Watch the images created by the swirling cream, and interpret the shapes as above.

There are literally hundreds of divination tools and techniques to choose from. For more ideas and instructions, read my book *FutureTelling: A Complete Guide to Divination*.

CHAPTER 2

Feeding the Heart and Soul

Familiarity breeds attempt.
                    —Goodman Ace

Something about delicious food arouses our passion for good company. Combining just the right magical atmosphere with enchanted food and drink can make love's job a lot easier. This chapter suggests ways of doing just that.

AMBIANCE FOR ROMANCE

If music be the food of love play on!
                    —Shakespeare

Music, colors, and decorations can create many different moods, often using the same basic ingredients. For example, candles and flowers are suited for either romantic or friendly settings. What determines the particular significance is the color, shape, and scent of the candles, or the color and type of flowers.

Use the guides below to design an atmosphere that matches your heart's intent, along with your magical recipes.

Candle Magic

The color, shape, aroma, and placement of a candle helps delineate its magical purpose. In choosing colors, look to the list on page 30 for ideas. For shapes, notice what immediately comes to mind when you see different candles. Round ones accent unity and fertility, square ones emphasize strong foundations, and heart-shaped ones energize all types of love magic just by association. (Also see the Shape Associations List, page 110.)

For scents, candles are more subtle than air fresheners, and easier on allergy sufferers. Either buy a pre-scented candle, or dab a little essential oil on it before lighting. Choose the oil according to the ideas presented in Chapter 3. As you dab on the oil or light the candle, consider adding an incantation such as,

For intimate evenings:

> *flame burn true, flame burn bright,*
> *kindle our love, our passion ignite.*

For friendship:

> *the light of kindness, the light of peace,*
> *let love in this friendship never cease.*

The placement of the candle(s) can also add meaning. For a romantic evening, put one next to the bed; for a quiet time of sharing, in the dining room or living room.

Clothing Magic

If clothes make a person, consider what signals your clothing conveys. If meeting a friend, wear something comfortable accented with a piece of jewelry or clothing he or she gave you. This symbolically reaffirms your connection to each other. For a date, wear colors that accent your mood. Bright hues are more playful; medium tones take the proverbial middle ground; and deep pigments indicate seriousness or intensity.

As you get dressed, visualize sparkling light being absorbed by your clothes. This will let your spiritual nature shine. You can also create incantations to go with your wardrobe. For example, bind energy into your tie saying, *With one love knot, forget me not.*

Or energize a dress, saying,

> *While in this dress, I'll look my best*
> *Love through me shine, true love be mine!*

If things turn out poorly, you can put your clothes in the laundry right away to remove any lingering negativity. This way you don't keep excess stress in the sacred space of your home.

Color Magic

Colors emit distinct vibrations that affect the way humans feel and behave. Watch the different energy level of a child playing in a room painted a bright color or a room painted a dark color. Chances are good the child will be more active in the presence of bright, life-affirming colors.

Color can accentuate your magical ambiance, blatantly or subtly. Trust your instincts and refer to the following list for choosing specifically colored accents—from flowers and table settings to candles and light bulbs.

Color List

Red—energetic, passionate, vibrant, earnest
Pink—friendly, playful, sociable
Orange—magnanimous, generous, cordial
Yellow—warm, considerate, creative, harmonious
Green—productive, progressive, fertile
Blue—quiet, mysterious, thoughtful, peaceful
Purple—whimsical, spiritual, mystical
Brown—constructive, grounded
Black—restful, serious, solemn
White—protective, cleansing, pure

Imagine you are meeting a friend with whom you have recently had an argument. You might want to include white and blue in your accent colors to encourage ethical, peaceful vibrations, and perhaps some pale purple flowers to inspire playfulness, and green foliage so the meeting is productive.

Decoration Magic

Details can be powerful, and it's often the subtle ornamental touches that make an impact during a rendezvous. For example, I have a friend who incorporates Eastern philosophy into his personal path. Once, when seeing him after a long period apart, I designed an Eastern-themed meal for him, complete with a low-level table, pillows, sandalwood incense, Japanese fans, and chopsticks. He really appreciated the effect. Remember that thoughtfulness is a kind of magic all its own.

One effective decorating idea is to place candles, crystals, objects, or herbs in the four directional points corresponding to the four elements. Here are two examples of how this might work:

For a romantic engagement:

> *South*—a red candle for the fire element, and for passion

> *West*—an amethyst for the water element, balancing passion with sensitivity

> *North*—a bowl of primrose petals for the earth element , encouraging a peaceful, respectful evening

East—a wind chime for the element air, inspiring harmony

For a reunion with a friend:

South—a yellow candle for the fire element, stimulating interesting, energetic discourse

West—a bowl of simmering lemon potpourri for the water element, encouraging cordial emotions

North—two turquoise stones for the earth element, generating friendship with firm foundations (When your friend leaves, give him/her one stone as a memento to keep you close spiritually.)

East—a picture of the two of you placed near a window for the air element, inspiring a fresh beginning

By setting up the meeting place in this way, you've also created an informal sacred circle. This circle can be augmented magically using an invocation or verse while you set out the objects. Any personal invocation you have for calling the four quarters, or an incantation for empowering objects will work. If possible, try to make the verse specific to your purpose and the items represented.

An invocation for the second example might follow this pattern:

> East—*Powers of the East, witness my friend and me together with joyful hearts. Renew that joy today.*
> Put up the picture.
>
> South—*Powers of the South, witness our reunion and reignite the spark of our friendship today.*
> Light the candle.
>
> West—*Powers of the West, witness our hearts and let them sing together friendship's song today.*
> Put the lemon in the simmering pot.
>
> North—*Powers of the North, witness us. Energize these stones to enhance our connection, our unity, and our steadfast friendship.*
> Put out the stones.

In these examples, the movement around the meeting space should be clockwise for positive, growth-oriented energy. If you're meeting someone in order to break up or clear the air, you may wish to move counterclockwise to decrease or banish undesired attentions and negativity.

Musical Magic
Music is the universal language. It can express many things for which words are inadequate. During my musical studies, I've

discovered a few generalities about the message communicated by certain instruments:

- Brass instruments can be romantic, whimsical, or thoughtful, depending on the piece.

- Drums are passionate and energizing for almost everyone. Lovers' hearts tend to beat along with music featuring drums alone or music with a strong percussion line.

- Flutes or lutes have traditionally been used to play the music of love in many cultures.

- Horns are excellent for celebratory occasions.

- Strings are best suited to romance or quiet discussions.

- Lyrics can be meaningful when played at intimate moments, but distracting if played at full volume during conversation.

Since musical tastes vary greatly, these generalizations can't be taken as hard and fast rules. Bear in mind what you and your companion enjoy, and the focus of the meeting. Some New Age music is especially effective for creating a magical atmosphere without being obtrusive.

THE FOOD OF LOVE

There is an art to cooking that can make any meal, even macaroni and cheese, into an appetizing, seductive dish. If the way to the heart is through the stomach, then add magic to the mixture for a helpful nudge.

The difference between everyday edibles and magical meals depends on your attitude. Approaching your kitchen with a respectful, spiritual outlook affects the energy the food absorbs. Beyond this, here are some preparatory hints to magically empower your love-centered foods:

- Consider ingredients for their magical symbolism. Mix and match those best suited to your goals and the dish being prepared (see Appendix A). Consider side dishes and beverages, too. Nearly every edible item has been given a mystical correspondence at some point in history. Use this association, or, better yet, personal significance, in choosing your menu.

- Choose ingredients with the colors that represent your goals, or visualize them being filled with colored light. With some foods, like cookies, you can add food coloring to the mixture to increase the magic.

- Add magically charged herbs to a recipe as long as the flavor isn't detrimental to the dish (otherwise consider a tincture).

- When you want a subtle approach to vibrationally enhanced foods and beverages, try adding a few drops of Bach's Flower Essences. These essences are designed to affect the energies, characteristics, or outlook of the person consuming them as follows:

  Increasing tolerance—Beech
  Increasing trust—Holly

Increasing perseverance—Oak
Increasing commitment—Scleranthus
Increasing interest—Wild rose
Decreasing fear—Cherry plum
Decreasing possessiveness—Chicory
Decreasing egotism or self-involvement—Heather
Decreasing oppressiveness—Vine
Decreasing bitterness or anger—Willow

Flower essences have no flavor, so they will not alter your recipes in any way.

- Prepare your food during auspicious astrological hours or days. It can always be frozen until needed.

- Use a numerically significant number of courses or ingredients. For example, two main dishes can symbolize partnership.

- Stir mixtures clockwise to draw positive energies.

- Stir counterclockwise to banish negative energies.

- Keep a strong image of your goal in mind while you work.

- Cook with joy and love in your heart.

- Pray, chant, or incant over your food while preparing it.

- Eat expectantly, internalizing the energy created.

For more ideas and recipes along these lines, see my books *A Kitchen Witch's Cookbook* and *Witch's Brew*.

Friendship Foods

The foods for friendship should be warm, welcoming, and cozy. They should inspire happy memories and associations of your present relationship or characteristics you would wish for in new friends.

Potential friendship foods and their associations include:

Almonds—restoring friendship
Apples—peace, love
Berries—joy
Bread—kinship
Butter—healing emotional wounds
Caraway—trust
Cardamom—unity
Celery—grounding energy, tranquillity
Leeks—community spirit, common bonds
Lemon—steadfastness
Lentils—happiness, spiritual love
Lettuce—peaceful fellowship
Passion fruit—friendship, cordial feelings
Pineapple—hospitality, welcome
Rice—blessings, abundance
Sweets—life's sweetness

A friendship meal could begin with an appetizer of warm dill bread drizzled with melted cheese. The warmth of the loaf represents congenial feelings; the cheese and dill symbolize love. Next, enjoy a lentil soup and a tossed salad. Make sure to leave the lettuce leaves whole rather than cutting them, lest you cut off peace and prosperity. The main dish should appeal to the tastes of you and your companion. Top off the evening with mixed berries and passion fruit garnished with sweet cream to bring sweetness and happiness.

FRIENDSHIP RECIPE SAMPLER

Almond-Orange Butter

Magical Associations: Resolves problems between friends in a healthy, peaceful manner. Orange renews faith between people; spread on biscuits or rolls, it rekindles kinship.

> 1 cup sweet butter
> 1 teaspoon almond extract
> 2 teaspoons minced almonds
> 1/2 teaspoon orange extract
> pinch of sugar (optional)

Let the butter soften at room temperature for an hour, then beat it with the remaining ingredients until well blended. Spread the mix on your roll counterclockwise if trying to disperse negative feelings.

Friendship Fondue

Magical Associations: Strengthens common bonds. The creamy texture of the cheese enhances congruity in your relationship; the bread internalizes kinship.

3/4 pound cheese
1 tablespoon flour
2 cloves garlic, split
1 1/4 cup milk or half and half
salt and pepper to taste
1 loaf French bread, cubed

Cut the cheese into thin strips and coat them with the flour. Rub the garlic on the inside of the fondue pan. If you like garlic, leave the cloves in the pan for stronger flavor. Pour in the milk and let it warm, but do not boil. Slowly add the cheese. Stir constantly until completely integrated and smooth. Add salt and pepper, and enjoy. Yield: 5 to 6 servings

Leek Salad

Magical Associations: Improves rapport. The eggs accent fertile emotions; the yogurt establishes harmony; and tomatoes are often called "love apples."

> 1 leek
> 1 hard-boiled egg, chopped
> 2 ripe tomatoes, chopped
> 1/2 cup yogurt
> 1 tablespoon chopped chives
> 1/2 tablespoon olive oil
> 1/2 tablespoon lemon juice
> dash honey mustard

Clean the leek well; slice it thinly, then separate it into rings. Put it in a medium-sized bowl with the chopped egg and tomatoes. Put aside. In another bowl, mix the yogurt with the chives, oil, lemon juice, and mustard, then toss with the leek and egg. Garnish with carrot or green pepper slices, or sprigs of parsley. Yield: 2 servings

Pineapple Upside-down Cake

Magical Associations: Cultivates a sense of welcome and amiable gathering. Represents "turning over" a new leaf.

1/4 cup butter
2/3 cup brown sugar, well-packed
1 16-ounce can sliced pineapple, drained
Green and red maraschino cherries
1 1/3 cup self-rising flour
1 cup granulated sugar
1/3 cup shortening
1 teaspoon powdered ginger
1 teaspoon vanilla extract
3/4 cup milk
1 egg

Preheat oven to 350° F. Melt the butter in a 9-by-9-by-2 pan, sprinkling the brown sugar on top of the butter. Arrange the pineapple slices evenly on top of the sugar, adding the cherries to make a heart shape or other symbol you associate with kinship.

Mix the remaining ingredients slowly until well-blended (about 3 to 5 minutes on medium speed). Pour this into the pan and bake for 45 minutes. Test the center with a toothpick to see if the dough is completely cooked. Once it is out of the oven, immediately flip the cake onto a plate for serving. Enjoy hot or cold with a drizzle of sweet cream.

Romantic Rations

The foods for romance should tickle all the senses. The more pleasing a feast is to our eyes, nose, and mouth, the more likely it is to arouse romantic feelings. The only precaution here is not to cook overly heavy foods which might inspire napping instead.

Potential romance and love foods include those listed for friendship and:

Allspice—luck
Apricots—sentimental feelings
Barley—healing of a broken heart, inspiring loving feelings
Beets—passion
Berries—happy, playful romance
Brazil nuts—growing emotions
Brussels sprouts—stability
Cheese—fruition, harmony
Cinnamon—faithfulness, devotion
Guavas—fantasy
Honey—"sweet" feelings
Lamb—sensitivity
Orange—devotion, self-love
Peas—general love
Pumpkin seeds—increased interest
Quince—joy, contentment
Strawberries—happy love
Sweet potatoes—gentleness, kindness
Tomatoes—"love apples"

This particular grouping of foods is a vegetarian's dream come true. For a romantic rendezvous, begin with spiced pumpkin seeds to "spice things up." Move on to a sweet potato pie and perhaps a tomato salad. Then have strawberries tossed with chopped brazil nuts and sweet cream for dessert!

Cinnamon Rose Water Biscuits

Magical Associations: The cinnamon inspires devotion; the rose water emphasizes amorous feelings; and the sugar brings sweetness.

> 2 cups flour
> 1 teaspoon baking powder
> 3 tablespoons sugar
> 1/4 teaspoon salt
> 1 teaspoon cinnamon
> 3/4 cup milk
> 2 tablespoons honey
> 2 tablespoons rose water
> 1/3 cup oil
> flour (for kneading)

Mix all ingredients together, stirring until blended. If necessary, add a little more milk so that the dough forms easily into balls. Knead the dough on a floured surface, then roll it to 3/4 inches thick. Cut out biscuits with a heart-shaped cookie cutter and place on an ungreased cookie sheet about 1 inch apart. Bake in a preheated 450° F oven for about 12 minutes, until golden brown. Serve warm with a drizzle of honey. Yield: 1 dozen

Brussels Sprout-Cheese Soup

Magical Associations: The romance in this recipe comes from knowing your love is on solid ground (the Brussels sprouts) and filled with harmony (melted cheese).

> 2 tablespoons butter
> 1 onion, chopped
> 1 small potato, diced
> 2 cups Brussels sprouts,
>   trimmed and chopped
> 1 tablespoon flour
> 2 cups chicken stock
> 1 teaspoon garlic (optional)
> 1/2 cup heavy cream
> salt and pepper to taste
> grated cheese

Melt the butter and use it to sauté the onion and potato. Add the chopped Brussels sprouts. Cook for 5 minutes, stirring regularly. Add the flour, continuing to stir. Once the flour is incorporated, pour in the stock a little at a time. Add the salt and pepper, and simmer for half an hour. Transfer the soup to a blender and mix until smooth. Reheat with the cream, then serve with a garnish of grated cheese. Yield: 2 to 4 servings

Barbecued Strawberry Chicken

Magical Associations: Chicken encourages a healthy romance; strawberries, being sacred to Venus, encourage love, joy, and passion; honey adds pleasure.

Marinade:
4 to 6 pieces chicken
1 12-ounce can frozen
    strawberry daiquiri juice, thawed
1 tablespoon soy sauce
1 teaspoon powdered garlic
1 teaspoon powdered ginger

Barbecue Sauce (for about 3 pieces chicken):
1 cup honey
1 teaspoon powdered ginger
1 tablespoon chopped garlic
2 tablespoons crushed strawberries
    (optional)

Spear the chicken on both sides with a fork. In a sealable container, mix together the juice with the soy sauce, garlic, and ginger. Place the chicken in the marinade for 24 hours in the refrigerator, turning it regularly.

Stir the ginger, garlic, and strawberries into the honey. After the chicken has been turned once on the grill, begin basting the meat with the honey sauce. Continue turning and basting until golden brown. Garnish with fresh berries and a mint leaf.

Raspberry-Orange Scones

Magical Associations: Inspires playful romance, devotion, and healthy and abundant love.

2 1/2 cups flour
2 teaspoons baking powder
3/4 cup sugar
1 teaspoon baking soda
1/2 teaspoon salt
1/3 cup butter
1 egg, beaten
3 tablespoons orange juice
1/2 teaspoon grated orange rind
1/2 cup raspberries, diced

Mix the flour, baking powder, sugar, baking soda, and salt. Cut in butter to make a grainy meal. Add the egg, orange juice, and orange rind. Mix until all ingredients are blended. Shape 2 dozen balls from the dough. Place these on a greased cookie sheet about 1 inch apart, flattening them with the back of a spoon. Bake in a preheated 425° F oven for 15 minutes until browned. Serve covered with fresh berries and sweet cream.

Eros Edibles

Since the dawn of time people have looked to food and drink to inspire sexual interest and passion. Many of the foods listed for romance are suitable here as well as the following:

Asparagus—sexual prowess
Carrots—desire (Glaze them to make the encounter sweeter.)
Cashew—zeal
Celery—passion
Chocolate—love, adoration
Dill—exhilaration, endurance
Eggs—fertility
Figs—physical energy, passion
Licorice—enhancement of sexual experience
Mint—stimulation of physical interest
Olives—stress relief, arousal
Onion—increased energy
Sesame (with honey)—increased physical attractiveness and interest in sex
Shellfish—passion
Rice—improvement of sexual skill, fertility
Vanilla—loving energies and expressions

For a menu based on the above ingredients, begin with an Italian tomato salad with onions and chopped celery to tantalize the taste buds and the imagination. Move on to an asparagus quiche (for prowess and fertility), and top the meal off by feeding one another a chocolate cashew pie.

PASSIONATE RECIPE SAMPLER

Sensual Stuffed Olives

Magical Associations: Olives arouse desire from a foundation of love and respect; chives and garlic add zest.

> 1 can of "colossal" (extra large)
>   pitted black olives
> 6 ounces cream cheese
> 1 teaspoon baked garlic, minced
> 1 teaspoon garlic powder
> 2 teaspoons chives, minced
> 2 teaspoons green pepper, minced (optional)

Drain the olives completely and allow the cream cheese to soften. Blend the cheese with the baked garlic, garlic powder, chives, and green pepper until evenly mixed. Use a small knife to stuff the olives slightly above the top. Chill. Yield: 2 to 4 servings

Sesame Cashew Rice

Magical Associations: Increases attractiveness, desire, and physical staying power for intimate moments.

> 1 cup long-grain rice
> 2 bouillon cubes
>   (beef, chicken, or vegetable)
> 2 cups water
> 1 1/2 tablespoons cashew or sesame oil
> 1 tablespoon soy sauce
> 1/4 cup sesame seeds
> 1/4 cup cashews, chopped

Place the rice and bouillon in a pot with the water. Bring this to a boil, then reduce heat and simmer, covered, for 30 minutes or until tender. Cool.

Heat a wok with oil and cook the rice with the soy sauce and sesame seeds for five minutes. Stir in cashews and serve. Yield: 2 to 3 servings

Clams Piquant

Magical Associations: Entices passion filled with intense energy and warmth.

> 1 1/2 tablespoons butter
> 1/2 onion, minced
> 1/4 green pepper, minced
> 1 6.5-ounce can minced clams
> 1/2 cup grated cheese
> 1/2 tablespoon tomato purée
> 1/2 tablespoon garlic,
>   powdered or freshly chopped
> 1/2 tablespoon Worcestershire sauce
> 1/4 tablespoon soy sauce
> 2 slices rye toast

Melt the butter in a small frying pan. Sauté the onion and pepper in the butter. Next add the clams, cheese, tomato, garlic, Worcestershire, and soy sauce. Cook until the cheese mingles with the other ingredients. Serve on the rye toast, possibly with some fresh cheese as a garnish. Yield: 2 servings

Vanilla Creme

Magical Associations: Smoothes the way for sweet, loving, physical encounters.

> 1 tablespoon cornstarch
> 1/8 cup sugar
> 1 egg, beaten
> 1 1/2 cups milk
> 1/2 tablespoon butter
> 1 teaspoon vanilla extract

Mix cornstarch and sugar together and set aside. Blend the beaten egg and milk thoroughly, and cook over a low flame, slowly adding the cornstarch and sugar. Cook until the mixture thickens. Turn off the heat and fold in the butter and vanilla. Make sure the butter melts completely. Chill. For extra energy, garnish with a sprinkling of cinnamon. Yield: 2 to 3 servings

LOVE POTIONS

Historically, one of the most popular tools of the "hunt" has been the love potion, which makes the perfect beverage to accompany love's feast.

Friendship Beverages

These beverages can serve one of two purposes: they can open the way for new friendships or deepen existing friendships, just as foods do.

Potential components for friendship-stimulating beverages include:

Allspice—luck

Almond extract—wisdom, understanding

Apple—an all-purpose love juice or flavoring

Bay—heightened awareness and intuition when seeking new companions

Elder (water)—peace, wholeness

Fennel—protection from people who may not have your best interest at heart

Grape (juice or wine)—celebration

Lavender (water)—happiness

Lemon (juice or flavoring)—kinship, honesty

Mulberry (wine)—creative but practical exchanges

Passion fruit (juice)—the traditional fruit of friendship

Pineapple—deepened level of commitment

Strawberry (juice or flavoring)—light-hearted fun

FRIENDSHIP BEVERAGES RECIPE SAMPLER

Gingered Apple Juice

Magical Associations: Stimulates self-love. Since like attracts like, this will draw more potential companions to you.

> 1 cup apple juice (sparkling, if available)
> 1 teaspoon honey
> 1 quarter-inch piece candied ginger
> 1 allspice berry

The reason sparkling apple juice is preferred here is for uplifting energy. Warm the apple juice (for warm feelings), adding the honey and stirring until totally dissolved. Put the ginger and allspice in your favorite tea or coffee cup, pouring the honeyed juice over top. Drink whenever you need more self-confidence.

Strawberry-Pineapple Punch

Magical Associations: Encourages an abundance of good friends, warm feelings, fun, and hospitality.

> 12 whole frozen strawberries
> 1 cup pineapple chunks
> 1 1/2 cups strawberry juice
>   or 1/4 cup liqueur, if desired
> 1 liter ginger ale

Place the strawberries and pineapple chunks in a punch bowl with the strawberry juice or liqueur. Slowly pour in the ginger ale and stir clockwise.

Glogg

Magical Associations: The Swedish traditionally enjoy this beverage during the Yule season. Apples and almonds both enhance positive communication.

> 1 cup apple cider, wine, or mead
>   (honey wine) per person
> 1 whole clove per cup
> 1/2 cinnamon stick per cup
> 1/4 teaspoon almond flavoring per cup
> 1 slice apple per cup
> sweetening, as desired

Set out a cup for each person at the gathering. Warm the cider, wine, or mead in a pan with the cloves, cinnamon, and almond flavoring. Pour this into cups, garnishing each with an apple slice and a cinnamon stick to stir with.

Mulberry Wine

Magical Associations: Improves discernment in looking for, or communicating with, friends; increases appreciation and the intuitive nature.

> 5 pounds mulberries
> 1 gallon water
> 3 pounds sugar
> 1/2 orange, sliced, rind on
> 1-inch piece ginger root, bruised
> 1 tablespoon champagne yeast
> (now available at some supermarkets
> and brewery suppliers)

Mash the mulberries and stir them into the water in a nonaluminum pan. Let this steep overnight. Simmer mixture over a low flame for 1 hour, slowly adding sugar, and stirring regularly so the sugar dissolves completely. During the last 15 minutes, add the orange and ginger root. Let this cool to lukewarm.

In the meantime, suspend the champagne yeast in 1/4 cup warm water. Add this to the juice when it is lukewarm. Cover the pot with a heavy towel and let it sit for 48 hours undisturbed. Strain off the juice, pressing the berries to extract as much flavor as possible. Discard the berries. Leave the liquid in the pan again, covered, for 48 hours. Pour into glass containers with loose corks. Age for 3 weeks, then strain again, putting the wine into bottles with firm corks. Age in a dark, cool place for 1 year.

Romance and Love Refreshments

These refreshments may enhance an ongoing relationship, or spice up a new one. Since love thrives best when it isn't manipulated, only share these with people who are aware of what they're drinking. Otherwise, enjoy them yourself to internalize the magical attributes.

Potential components for romance and love refreshments include those listed for friendship, as well as the following:

Anise—longevity

Cardamom—a favorite Arabian herb for love and romance

Chamomile—reduced tension, so that romance can flourish

Cherry—playful love, fertility

Clove—a traditional love spice often appearing in ancient potion recipes

Currant—abundant, exciting romance

Ginger—energetic love and liaisons

Honey—happiness

Kiwi—uncomplicated, youthful love

Marjoram—safe, healthy relationships

Orange—devotion, fidelity, and luck

Plum—respectful adoration

Strawberry—light-hearted love, joy

Tea—peaceful, healthy relationships

Vanilla—zestful interest, admiration

Violet—charm, love, passion, and a little luck (it is edible)

ROMANTIC REFRESHMENT RECIPE SAMPLER

Apple-Berry Delight

Magical Associations: Brings energetic romance, dedication, compassion, and wisdom.

> 6 cups water
> 2 small red apples, unpeeled and sliced
> 1 orange, peeled and separated
> 1 one-inch slice lemon peel
> 1 cup raspberries
> 1/8 teaspoon ginger
> 1 cinnamon stick
> honey to taste

Put the water in a large pot with the fruit and herbs. Simmer over a low flame until the water turns dark red from the apple peels and the aroma is heady. Strain through cheesecloth, then sweeten with honey. Drink from a single cup to celebrate your unity.

Plum Mead

Magical Associations: Plums safeguard relationships from negativity, increase magnetic appeal, and help encourage longevity in love. Mead, or honey wine, is the beverage from which we get the word "honeymoon"—when couples celebrated their bond with 30 days of mead drinking.

> 25 large, ripe plums
> 1 gallon water
> 3 pounds honey
> 3 strands saffron
> 1 teaspoon rose water
> 1/2 orange, sliced, rind on
> 1 black tea bag
> 1/2 tablespoon wine or mead yeast
> (now available at some supermarkets
> and brewery suppliers)

Split and pit the plums, adding them to the water. Simmer for 30 minutes until the water is very red. Add honey, saffron, rose water, orange slices, and the tea bag. Bring this to a low, rolling boil, removing any scum that rises to the top over the next hour. Cool to lukewarm and strain.

While this cools, prepare your yeast by adding it to 1/4 cup of warm water and allowing it to work for 15 minutes. Stir this into the lukewarm juice and cover the pot with a heavy cloth. Leave for 7 days until the fermentation has slowed considerably. Strain again and pour the clear fluid into glass bottles. Adhere balloons with a rubber band to the tops of the bottles to allow the excess gas to escape. Remove the balloons after 8 weeks and cork tightly. Store in a dark, cool place for at least 6 months before using.

Note: If you need a beverage like this more quickly, plum wine is sold in liquor stores. You can warm it with symbolic spices before serving.

Kiwi-Strawberry Freeze

Magical Associations: Stimulates playful, light-hearted love and romance. While best suited to warm weather, this drink can also be enjoyed in front of a cozy fire.

> 2 kiwi fruits, peeled and diced
> 12 frozen whole strawberries
> 2 cups orange juice

Place the ingredients in a blender or food processor on the "frappé" setting. Blend until smooth and frothy. Serves 2.

Violet-Chamomile Cooler

Magical Associations: Decreases nervousness or anxiousness. Violets are ruled by Venus and represent enchantment.

1 quart spring water
1 orange, sliced, rind on
2 whole cloves
2 chamomile tea bags
1/2 cup violet petals, rinsed

Place all ingredients, except the violets, in a nonaluminum pan and heat. When the liquid is tepid (not yet boiling) add the violets and simmer until they become transparent. Strain and serve hot or cold with sweetener, as desired. A cold beverage accentuates keeping a "cool head" while a warm one emphasizes a "warm heart."

Passion Potions

Potions that encourage passion also make us feel good about ourselves and our lovers. The following magical ingredients inspire energetic interest, a sense of security, and intimacy between people who want a more titillating sexual relationship.

Potential components for passion potions include many for love and romance, since these feelings often go hand-in-hand. Other useful ingredients are:

Banana—improved male sexual prowess

Carrot (juice)—emphasized sexual nature

Coriander—heightened sexual enjoyment

Hazelnut—insight, fertility

Mango—excitement of romantic passion, especially for women

Milk—the lunar, romantic, mysterious self

Mint—lust

Peach—fertility balanced with wisdom

Pear—zeal, zest

Pomegranate—improved creativity in bed, fertility

PASSIONATE POTION RECIPE SAMPLER

Sweet Milk

Magical Associations: Enhances physical beauty when consumed or dabbed on the skin and hair. To attract a man, do this on Sunday, Tuesday, or Thursday. To attract a woman, on Monday or Friday. Cinnamon, sacred to Venus, is an aphrodisiac.

> 1 quart milk
> 1 cup honey
> 1 small cinnamon stick
> 1/2 teaspoon fennel

Warm all ingredients in a small saucepan until the honey is fully dissolved. Whip until frothy, then pour into cups. If desired, garnish with a bit of sweet cream and cinnamon sticks.

Banana-Mango Medley

Magical Associations: Balances yin-yang energy for mutually enjoyable physical encounters.

> 1 pint banana ice cream or frozen yogurt
> 1/2 cup ginger ale
> 1/2 cup mango juice
> 1 banana, sliced

Place ice cream, soda, and juice in a blender on a low setting. Slowly add the banana and continue blending until the beverage is smooth, like a milkshake. Enjoy with a garnish of whipped cream and cherries.

Peach and Pear Potion

Magical Associations: Helps a couple wishing to conceive out of a joyous, energetic love-making session.

> 2 cups pear juice
> 1 cup peach schnapps or juice
> 2 whole cloves
> 1/4 teaspoon hazelnut extract or flavoring
> 1 quarter-inch piece ginger root, bruised
> 2 nutmeg beans
> 1/4 teaspoon rose water

Warm all ingredients, except the rose water, in a small pan. Simmer until the liquid has a heady aroma. Strain and add the rose water, then serve warm or cold.

Metheglyn

Magical Associations: Metheglyn is a spiced mead often used for health purposes. It restores healthy sexual desire and enjoyment.

> 1 liter mead
> 3 whole cloves
> 1/4 teaspoon dried marjoram
> 1/2 teaspoon ground coriander
> 1 teaspoon mint
> 1/2 orange, peeled and sliced
> 1 teaspoon rose water

Warm the ingredients over low heat until the aroma of the herbs is full-bodied. Strain and serve warm with a fresh slice of orange or apple in each cup.

The potions in this chapter are a creative combination of historical lore, magical tradition, and imagination. I advocate trying your own modifications to make these elixirs as pleasing to the palate as they are meaningful. For more ideas for pantry love magic, refer to Appendix A.

CHAPTER 3

Scent-ual Love

"Purple the Sails, and so perfumed that the wind was love-sick with them."
—Shakespeare, *Antony and Cleopatra*, Act II, Scene 2

Our ancestors considered incense, perfumes, and other aromatics an important part of religious observance. Solomon felt that pomades (scented creams) rejoiced the heart, and Mohammed encouraged the use of aromatics among his followers. Greek writings describe many gods and goddesses as anointed, or sprinkled with fragrant oils. Anything that so pleased the gods must also have pleased their devout followers!

Perfumery was a common occupation in Moses' time. Scents were mysterious and exotic, and those who could afford them were regarded similarly as mysterious and exotic creatures. Aromatics were also thought to be healthful. This belief is possibly accurate, considering that medieval workers in French perfumeries showed a drastically lower incidence of plague than their neighbors.

In some cultures, perfume making was a sacred art, performed by priests and priestesses. Some aromas healed, others banished ghosts and curses. Still others were considered magically potent for pleasing, teasing, and increasing attractive energies.

The human need to feel handsome or beautiful is strongly connected to love's quest. Aromatics are one way we can affect how others perceive us, and how we perceive ourselves and the way we carry ourselves. A scent creates and expresses an auric beauty that is more than skin deep. With a little magic, we can accentuate inner attractiveness and, in turn, our potential to love and be loved.

In working with each of these recipes, feel free to experiment, but always record any changes you see so you don't lose the keys to favorite combinations. Remember, magic always flows better when you align it with your own personality, spiritual path, and personal agenda.

If possible, create these aromas at astrologically auspicious times, and remember to visualize your goals strongly as you work. Samples of chants and incantations are included to help energize the atmosphere, along with a list of potential ingredients that accentuate love's quest.

A WORD TO THE WISE

Making homemade aromatics may take a little practice before achieving satisfying results. The way herbs and flowers integrate depends on several factors including heat, light, exposure, the amount of aromatic oil in the plant, any mold or dirt present, and the tools used, to name a few. Be patient, recognizing that an unacceptable aroma may not have been your fault.

Start with very simple compounds. Don't use more than two or three aromatics at a time and notice how they blend. Fewer components in a recipe doesn't lessen the magic. In fact, it allows you to concentrate more fully on your goal. As you become more adept, your blends can become more elaborate.

While it might be tempting to try many products at once, this is a long journey. The skills acquired in perfecting each product will flow into your next effort.

Remember, skin allergies may make you or your companions sensitive to certain preparations. Check with your loved ones to see which ones they have an adverse reaction to. Test each preparation by dabbing a little on the back of your hand and letting it dry. If any itching or redness results, do not use—rashes won't help love or romance one bit.

BASIC AROMATIC COMPONENTS

Beauty—lavender, rosemary, mint, thyme

Communication—almond, bergamot, anise, mint

Decreased negativity—lemon rind, frankincense, myrrh

Departure (banishing)—bay, clove, mint, rosemary, mugwort, pine, vetiver

Love—apple, lemon, rose, dill, mace, clove, ginger

Passion—cinnamon, mint, patchouli, allspice, orange, violet, vanilla, dill

Stability—honeysuckle, patchouli, magnolia

Depending on the application, use whole herbs, powdered herbs, herb rinds, or herbal oils...whichever is most appropriate to the recipe and your time constraints.

Air Fresheners

Begin with a cup of beeswax to which you add 1/4 cup finely powdered herbs and 5 to 10 drops of essential oil(s). Let this cool, stirring periodically until you can handle the warm wax in your hand. Shape the wax around a wick in the shape of a heart or other significant emblem, adding an incantation that mirrors your goal, such as the following examples.

For romance:

> *Heart of my hearts, love of my love,*
> *be blessed by the Powers above.*
> *Where these aromas play and dance,*
> *create the spirit of romance!*

For a happy home:

> *As the sun warms this heart, negativity depart.*
> *Warm my home, and all within; by my will, the*
> *magic begins.*

Let the wax finish cooling, then hang the charm in a sunny window so it releases its aroma. After the wax loses its scent completely, use it as a love candle.

Baths

The Romans were among the first people to raise bathing to an art form. The Roman baths were lavish and typically scented with lavender.

Aromatic baths can be made very simply by steeping herbs bundled in a sachet in the hot bath water. Or, you can mix dried herbs and aromatic oils with sea salt or Epsom salts for greater benefits. Add ingredients a little at a time until the aroma is pleasing. You can also add food coloring to the salt for enhanced magical properties.

While you bathe, relax and allow the worries of the day to dissolve. Visualize your goal in as much detail as possible and let your aura absorb the energy of the herbs. Carry that energy with you through the day or evening.

Note: You can put a tea made from any herb suggested into your washing machine to imbue your clothing with the same energies and to accentuate the overall effect.

Breath Fresheners

"'Tis her breathing that perfumes the chamber."
—Shakespeare, *Cymbeline*, Act I, Scene 2

It's hard to be kissable when your breath smells of fish, coffee, garlic, or other strong food. Having magically charged breath fresheners can certainly give romance a boost. Two natural breath fresheners, mint leaves and ginger root, are also symbolically aligned with love's goal. Ginger root in candied form makes a refreshing sweet; mint leaves can be chewed just as they are.

If neither is available, buy spearmint-flavored breath fresheners or toothpicks, and energize them using an incantation such as,

> Let words linger sweetly on my lips
> and none by you be missed.
> Let desire linger gently in the air
> and bring about a kiss!

Candles
Candlelight sets the mood for love and romance; candles can also impart aroma into the atmosphere. Rather than making your own candles, which can be time-consuming, you can dab a little aromatic oil on a candle with a scent that matches your magical goal. Gently rub a couple of drops on the surface of the wax, adding an invocation such as,

> While this burns, so too my heart.
> Through this room, romance impart.

Change the word "romance" to other suitable words like "love" or "peace." (See Chapter 2 for more candle magic ideas.)

Carpet Fresheners
Carpet fresheners can enhance the ambiance of an entire room. They also make perfect cleansers to banish any unwanted lingering energies.

Begin with a cup of baking soda. Add 1 teaspoon each of powdered lemon rind, powdered orange rind, and ground allspice. Sprinkle this onto the carpet, saying,

Sprinkle magic all about.
Love goes in, negativity goes out!

Leave the mixture on the rug for 10 to 15 minutes, then vacuum it up. Many herbs will work as carpet fresheners, but should be in a fine powdered form for best results.

Creams

Aromatic creams are more than mere skin conditioners. They can be added to bath water, dabbed on light bulbs, or rubbed into wood (specifically in clothing drawers).

Basic Cream Recipe

2 parts vegetable oil
1 part herb (strain)
1/4 teaspoon benzoin powder
(as a fixative)
1 part beeswax

Warm the oil in a pan that you won't need for cooking again. Add the herb, benzoin, and wax, and stir until the wax is melted. Strain and let the blend cool until a film forms on the surface. Beat the mixture by hand until it has cooled completely. The result will be similar to cold cream. Remember to stir clockwise for positive energy, counterclockwise for banishing negativity. This is an excellent time to add a chant such as,

> *Round and round, the wheel it turns,*
> *within my heart, desire burns.*
> *Round again, to where love dwells,*
> *so begins my magic spell.*

Keep repeating this until you're finished making the cream. If the cream is too stiff, simply rewarm it and add 1 to 2 tablespoons more oil, and beat again until cooled. Store in an airtight container. Anytime you notice the cream losing its aroma, stir in a few drops of essential oil to refresh it.

Incense

Soft roll your incense, herbs and fruits and flowers in mingled clouds.

—James Thomson

Incense was among the first aromatics used regularly for religious purposes. It appeared in temples as an offering to the gods and goddesses of ancient cultures, such as those in Egypt, Rome, and Japan, just to name a few. The Grecian oracles and other seers used specially prepared incense to help create an altered state of consciousness where they could receive divine insights. In other settings people would sit near the smoke from fires filled with incense to purify and perfume themselves.

Traditionally, smoke generated by incense represents prayers and wishes rising to the heavens. As the wind moves the smoke, these desires are conveyed to the earth, to other people, the universe, and Spirit. Each ingredient changes the vibrational quality of the smoke, depending on its mystical characteristics.

In its simplest form, incense consists of finely ground, dried herbs. Powdered aromatic wood, dried fruits, honey, wine, and essential oils can also be added to this base.

Basic Incense Recipe
1 cup powdered wood
   (sandalwood, cedar, or pine)*
1/4–1/2 cup dried herb(s)
up to 12 drops essential oil
1 teaspoon orris root or benzoin powder
   (as a fixative)
1 to 2 teaspoons honey, wine,
   or aromatic water

*I have had some success in making finely ground wood using a good-sized pencil sharpener and slim pieces of the suggested woods.

Mix the wood powder, dried herbs, and fixative together in an earthenware dish. Equally disperse the essential oils and other ingredients over the top of this, stirring and folding constantly until well-blended. Leave this mixture out in the open air (so no mold grows) until completely dry. Then put it in a dark, airtight container and store it in a cool place. This incense requires self-lighting charcoal to burn, and is effective in very small amounts (e.g., 1/2 teaspoon). Some blends to consider for love include:

Blessing—red sandalwood base with cinnamon, bay, frank-incense, wine, and honey

Commitment—cedar base with cinnamon, juniper, and frank-incense

Communication—pine base with lavender and wormwood

Decreased negativity—sandalwood base with dill, frank-incense, sage, nutmeg, rosemary, myrrh, and fern

Departure (banishing)—cedar base with rue, fennel, and dill

Faithfulness—pine base with linden flower, basil, bayberry, and clove

God aspect (for men)—sandalwood base with bay, myrrh, cinnamon, ginger, patchouli, and ginger

Goddess aspect (for women)—cedar base with cinnamon, violet, vetiver, and rose

Loving home—juniper wood base with orange, rose, basil, dragon blood, gardenia, and lavender

Luck in love—cedarwood base with allspice and clove. Add a dried four leaf clover or a five-petaled lilac, if you have one.

Passion—sandalwood base with musk, dragon blood, saffron, and carnation

Promises—sandalwood base with mace and pine needles

Romance—sandalwood base with jasmine, gardenia, lotus, bay, and rose

You can delete any herb in the above combinations and/or replace it with something more pertinent to your situation. Tint the final product with a little food coloring, or store a few sympathetic crystals (see Appendix A) in the jar for increased meaning, improved magical focus, and augmented power.

Oils

The ancients originally used aromatic oils for religious purposes, specifically for anointing themselves before entering sacred spaces. The oil blessed the priest/ess or petitioner, and pleased the gods. Today, magically empowered oils can serve as signature colognes, perfumes, room fresheners, light bulb and candle aromatics, bath oils, auric massage oils, flavored cooking oils, anointing oils for amulets, and so on.

To make your own aromatic oils, you need a good quality base with a texture you enjoy. Almond oil, virgin olive oil, and safflower oil all have a long shelf life, a lightweight body, and are edible so you can use them in preparing love's foods (see Chapter 2).

The traditional method for making an aromatic oil is to steep herbs in a base oil. Begin with one handful of herbs or flower petals, and cover completely with warmed oil. Steep for 48 hours in sunlight. Strain and repeat, adding more herbs or petals until you like the intensity. Bottle and label for storage in a cool, dark place. Individually infused oils can be blended for greater potency and magical meaning.

If time is short, add essential oils to the base oil, a drop or two at a time, until you get a pleasing scent. Twirl the ingredients clockwise (for positive energy), or counterclockwise (to banish negativity). Some good blends to consider are:

Attraction—patchouli and clove

Blessing—cinnamon, myrrh, and a touch of saffron

Decreased negativity—rose, gardenia, lavender, and orange

Departure (banishing)—rosemary, lily, and vervain

Energy—pine, lemon, mint, clove, and sage

God aspect (for men)—musk, patchouli, cinnamon, ambergris, clove, and allspice

Goddess aspect (for women)—gardenia, rose, jasmine, lotus, and violet

Heartache—basil, marjoram, and rosemary

Loving home—bergamot, lavender, clove, musk, and vanilla

Passion—musk, frankincense, patchouli, pine, cedar, vanilla, jasmine, and coriander

Romance—sandalwood, lemon, rose, and vanilla

Store your oils in glass containers with airtight lids, away from heat and light. If they turn cloudy, discard them. This indicates the oil has gone rancid and the magical quality is tainted.

Perfumes/Colognes

The ancient Egyptians, Greeks, Romans, and Arabs were all advocates of perfume. The Roman noblemen went so far as to use different perfumes for different body parts, including mint on their arms and marjoram on their hair. The Arabs finally introduced the art of perfume distillation to Europe in the sixteenth century, where it flourished in Italy, France, and England. Perfume became associated with lovesickness, a malady caused by the bewitching magic of scents.

France was and still is the heart of the perfume industry. During the Renaissance, perfume became highly fashionable and all manner of perfume-scented items, from gloves to pomanders, were manufactured there. The ancient lore of perfume's magical powers has not been lost. Napoleon bathed his head in cologne before any military campaign to assure his success.

A perfume acts as a personal marker. It accentuates how you feel and hints at your intentions, giving love an opportunity to find you by attracting similar energy.

Commercially produced brands are very difficult to duplicate at home. A simpler method is to mix 1/4 cup rubbing alcohol, 1/4 cup witch hazel tincture, and 1/2 cup water. Add essential oil(s) to this mixture and shake. If time isn't an issue, steep whole herbs instead of essential oils in the mixture until the aroma becomes heady. Strain and pour into a bottle with a spray cap.

Before applying, use visualization or incantation to empower the symbolic elements. Always shake well before using. The action of shaking can also activate the magical energy.

Potpourri

Cleopatra sprinkled her floor with rose petals before Marc Anthony's arrival, hoping the aroma would encourage his love. The strewing of flowers, leaves, and aromatic herbs has historically marked festival days in churches and at public celebrations. It is to this tradition that potpourri owes its origins.

Potpourri begins with chopped pieces of aromatic plants, such as bark, flower petals, fruit peels, or tree resins. Mix and match these ingredients, then add essential oils to intensify the aroma. Some examples include:

Devotion—magnolia petals, nutmeg beans, lemon peel

Joyful relationship—lavender flowers, dried morning glories, spearmint leaves, orange rind

Love—whole dried roses, cinnamon sticks, apple peel

Passion—cinnamon sticks, dried daisies, hibiscus petals, violet petals, and violet-scented oil

Pure intentions—French lavender flowers, vervain, coconut-scented oil

You can enhance the warmth of your love magic by simmering the potpourri. As you heat the herbs, add an incantation such as,

> *Love is gentle, love is warm,*
> *through this blend let love be born.*

Simmer for as long as you like, adding extra water as needed to avoid burning.

Powders

To make a scented body powder, begin with a base of cornstarch, baking soda, arrowroot, or unscented talc. To each cup
of base powder add approximately 10 drops of essential oil and
up to 1/2 cup powdered herb. Keep this mixture in a sealed
container and mix it regularly for two weeks. Each time you
shake the mixture, add an incantation such as,

> *Let the magic within, begin, begin.*
> *Generate love and peace, let it never cease,*
> *When sprinkled around, romance abounds.*
> *When in my shoe, passion pours through.*
> *Let the magic within, begin, begin.*

After two weeks, sift the mixture with a flour sifter or fine
mesh wire. This will separate out any large pieces, leaving you
with a fine powder for use on the skin.

Sachets

Sachets were called "sweetbags" during the Middle Ages.
Sachets can be placed inside dream pillows, bundles for clothing
drawers, pincushions, and so on. (See Chapter 5 for examples of
portable sachets.)

The beauty of sachets lies in their simplicity. Begin with a
piece of cloth that is large enough to be gathered and tied
around a handful of herbs. Choose a color aligned with your
magical goal. Place the dried herbs and a little essential oil in

the middle of the cloth, and tie it with colored ribbon or string. That's all there is to it.

For a lover's dream pillow, use jasmine petals, marigold petals, rose petals, and balsam needles. To create a romance bundle for clothing drawers, try basil, cloves, rose oil, lavender, lemon peel, and orange peel. For a pincushion that will draw passion to you, combine cinnamon, mint, rosemary, and violet petals. Other potential sachet blends include:

Departure (banishing)—dill, vervain, rue, salt, fennel, and basil

Healing a broken heart—allspice, apple, lemon balm, cedar, mint, thistle, and willow

Love—rose, orange, baby's breath, angelica, hibiscus, rosemary, and lemon verbena

Luck in love—allspice, heather, nutmeg, orange rind, rose, and violet

Peace—chamomile and lavender

Soaps

Soaps naturally engender a feeling of freshness and cleanliness. In love magic, this association translates to cleaning, refreshing, and energizing our auras. Soap can also wash away any self-doubt, tension, or other concerns, replacing them with positive magic.

Making soap at home is somewhat labor-intensive. Instead, I suggest buying an unscented soap and adding the aroma to it.

Start with a wooden box lined with a linen or cotton cloth. Dab 1 to 3 essential oils on the cloth, then lay the unwrapped soap in the box. Fold the cloth over the soap and sprinkle on some more oil. Cover the box and let it sit for one month. Soap is porous and will slowly absorb the scent.

Each day as the soap sits, visualize the box being permeated with reddish-pink light (colors of love), and say something like,

> Within this soap, my magic bind.
> A true love, I soon shall find.
> Away all fears, all insecurity erased
> Within my aura, by confidence replaced.

As with any incantation, change the words to express your intentions, making sure you feel comfortable when you say them. Some choices for love soaps include:

Auric cleansing and balance—coconut oil soap with lemon
Body beautiful—avocado soap with lily and geranium oil
Negativity chaser—white soap with vetiver and wintergreen
Personal passion—white soap with cinnamon, mint, and
    vanilla
Sensitivity and intuition—aloe soap with sandalwood and
    honeysuckle oil

Waters
Scented waters can be made quickly almost anywhere, as long as you have hot water and a suitable aromatic. Waters have a

variety of applications, including magical finger bowls, rinse cycle clothing refreshers, after-bath spritzers, hair rinses, teas, and food and beverage enhancers.

A good proportion for herb and flower waters is 1/2 ounce of herb to 2 pints of water. Some blends to consider for your love magic include the following:

Beauty—May dew with rose water. Gather the dew by putting out a clean, thick cloth at night and wringing it out into a container before the sun rises the next morning. Traditionally, the most powerful day to do this is Beltane (May 1).

Faithfulness—vervain water dabbed on your forehead, heart, and feet. This keeps your mind and heart on your beloved, and keeps your feet from straying.

Lusty love—caraway, dill, and rosemary seed steeped with violet, vanilla, or rose

Success in love—red rose petals steeped with juniper

Wisdom—sage water steeped with sunflower petals

Store aromatic waters in the refrigerator as they have a short shelf life. If the water becomes cloudy, discard it and make a fresh batch.

CHAPTER 4

Love Spells

"Our state of being matters to those around us, so we need to become conscious of what we unintentionally share so we can learn to share with intention."
—Peggy T. Millin, *Mary's Way*

Magic can keep love alive and fresh, enhancing our inherent charms. We must be responsible, however, and not turn love spells and potions into a game. They are serious business and can act as an astral road map to guide the right person into your life.

Several ingredients are necessary to creating reliable love magic. The first is faith—in your magic and yourself. Without faith, magic becomes an exercise in futility. The second is intention. Without purpose and direction, magical energy disperses back to the source.

The third part of the equation is detachment. Detach yourself from preconceived notions of Mr. or Ms. "Right." Allow the universe to open its possibilities to you. Detach yourself from your physical ideal and concentrate on the emotional qualities you want in a mate. Love begins in the heart, not your eyes—and sometimes what you see is not what you get.

Also, once you've completed it, detach the magic itself. Without this release, like a tethered balloon, the energy will never fly. Then let go of any possessiveness; love will not survive any clinging. Lastly, detach yourself. Get out and socialize, and give the universe a chance to fulfill your needs.

If you're using love magic to draw a mate, you may still meet a few toads before finding that prince or princess. If you're using it to improve an established relationship, use honesty as your tinder to get those sparks burning.

SEEKING LOVE

Love seems to play hide-and-seek with those actively pursuing it. And the rules of the game constantly change according to social and personal attitudes. This makes the quest a challenge, but one which spellcraft can meet successfully. The only caution here is to remember that you are responsible for any relationship that develops as a result of magical fostering.

Relationships are intricate and delicate. Magic will not, in itself, make or break a potential or ongoing relationship. It simply provides a nudge or spark. The rest is up to you.

Clearing Love's Path

Love's road is often full of blocks and potholes. A little magic, however, can clear the way. Begin by bathing in carnation petals and bay leaves. This dispels negativity and makes you more open to receiving love. Then write your wish for love on a piece of parchment, visualizing pink light saturating the paper. Take this outside at midnight, and concentrate on any single star, saying,

> *Oh star, whose silver light ignites my wish a'fire,*
> *grant me my heart's desire!*
> *Make clear the way for finding love.*
> *Bless this wish from up above.*

Wear the paper in your left shoe until the magic manifests, then burn it with thankfulness.

Love Thyself

Before others can love you, you must learn to love yourself. This is hard because we are often our own worst critics. But to foster love, it has to start within. To help accomplish this, bless an apple, saying three times, *Fruit of wholeness, be filled with confidence and love.* Eat the apple and begin internalizing loving self-acceptance, then plant the seeds so this positive image can grow.

Attracting More Love

To help bring a little more love into your life, anoint a pink or red candle with an aromatic oil of your choice (see Chapter 3 and Appendix A). Then tack the center of the candle with a rose thorn. Blend some silver glitter with rose petals and take the mixture and candle to your threshold. To attract a man, perform this spell on a Friday; to attract a woman, work on Tuesday.

Stand at your threshold and light the candle. Adhere it to the floor nearby so your hands are free. Walk outside, a few paces from your doorway, and begin sprinkling the glitter and petals on your walkway, saying,

> *Follow the light to me.*
> *I release love to the winds so it can return.*
> *Within my heart, this candle always burns.*

If possible, let the candle burn out naturally. Alternatively, burn it inside near the hearth (a fireplace or stove) each night before you go to sleep. When the candle melts to the point where the thorn falls out (this symbolically releases energy toward your goal), save the wax remnants with any remaining glitter, and carry them as a charm to draw love into your life.

Magnetic Appeal Glamoury

A glamoury creates a personal atmosphere which expresses your desires and desirability. The easiest method is to set up your bathroom for a luxury soak. Put on some empowering music, light candles, burn incense, and bathe in lavishly scented water. Visualize the water as sparkling light. Let this energy fill your aura; release any tensions. As you do, softly chant something such as,

> *Negativity at bay; worries washed away.*
> *Let the beauty within shine without.*
> *Erase all fears, all self-doubt,*
> *so all others see, is the beauty that's me!*

Repeat this until your voice grows louder from the energy created. Keep that energy with you after the bath.

Moon Glamoury

According to an old English custom, the moon can improve one's image. Stand beneath a waxing crescent moon and say,

> *Silver moon, magic moon, shine in my hair,*
> *silver moon, bright moon, magic to me bear,*
> *silver moon, magic moon, make me fair!*

Repeat this phrase each time you see the moon until it reaches fullness. The magic will begin manifesting then, and others will find you more attractive.

Drawing a Lover

When you're looking for someone with whom to share intimate moments, but not necessarily a lifetime, try this spell. Make two poppets (small cloth figurines) out of cloth dabbed with patchouli oil, and stuff them with verbena, vervain, yarrow, and rose petals. Set one across the room from the other on the first night of a waxing moon. Place a deep red or purple candle near your bed.

Each night, light the candle, saying this incantation three times, *Draw me to my lover; draw us close to one another.* Afterward, physically move the dolls closer together. On the night of the full moon, have the dolls meet. Bind them loosely (so the magic doesn't constrain) with a white ribbon and store them under your bed until the magic manifests. Keep the poppets as long as you maintain the relationship. When the two of you part, take off the binding and either burn or bury the dolls so only positive energy is left of that relationship.

Drawing a Life Mate

If you are looking for someone for a long-term relationship, an acorn can become your potent symbol. In ancient proverbs, this represented prolonged effort that lead to achievement. Plant an acorn in rich soil where it has room to grow, while strongly visualizing your wish for lasting love. Tend this with as much care as you would a relationship. When the acorn has taken root and begins sprouting, some potential partners should make themselves known.

This spell can easily be altered for fertility. Bind the acorn to an ear of corn before burying, and whisper your wish for a child to the acorn. Then tend it similarly.

Deterring a Rival

Is someone perpetually standing in the way of your relationships? Go to an area of mud or dirt, such as a park, where your rival has been walking. When they leave the area, rub out one of their footprints, saying,

> Turn away from what I love,
> may your interest disappear
> as this footprint from the earth.

If it be for the greatest good, and harm none
by my will, this spell's begun.

The fourth line of this incantation is very important. It keeps the magic from being manipulative and aligns your intention with that of the universe. Sometimes what appears as interference is really in our best interest.

DEEPENING LOVE
The level of commitment in a relationship—be it with a friend, lover, or potential life mate—can benefit from a magical boost. However, make sure your partner is as interested as you are in taking this step. Otherwise, magic can become manipulative or sticky with possessiveness.

Commitment
Commitment can apply to jobs, animals, and people, so this spell can be altered to fit the circumstance. Begin with a picture or personal item that represents the person or situation which you feel needs greater commitment. Hold this in your hands on the first night of a full moon. Visualize a red string extending from your heart chakra to this person or situation. Do not "glue" this to them, just offer it. Over the next two nights, repeat the visualization beneath the moon's beams. As you do, add an incantation to empower the visualization, such as,

From my heart to _____
(fill in with person/situation),

> *I offer a working partnership, a sharing.*
> *If this be your desire,*
> *take hold this string, and begin caring.*

Keep the picture or object with you as a charm. It will help manifest this commitment if it's meant to be.

Tolerance

No matter how much we love someone, sometimes it's hard to like everything about them. This spell will help you overlook the little things and focus on what's really important.

Leave an orange beneath the light of a waxing moon for 1 to 2 nights, charging the fruit with insight and perspective. On the next night, peel it. Exchange slices with your partner for kindness, respect, understanding, and faith in love. Eating the orange will internalize this energy as a promise to each other.

If you have to perform this spell alone, leave half of the orange slices out on the last night as an offering, inviting the other person's energy into your sacred space.

Unity

Two people do not enter into oneness overnight, sometimes not even over a lifetime. This spell will develop unity between people. Begin by making each other a braided bracelet of red, blue, and yellow string and some strands of your hair. Along the bracelet, tie three knots saying,

In this gift, love, trust, and insight combine.
With this thread my magic wind.
Within the knot, my love I bind.

Exchange your bracelets during the second night of a full moon, tying them on with three knots, symbolizing body, mind, and soul in harmony. If you can't easily wear a bracelet at the workplace, consider tying it around your ankle, or put it inside a wallet or other item that you carry regularly.

Harmony with In-laws

Even the best relationship suffers when the couple's two families are at odds. This spell will help in-laws to be more tolerant of each other. Begin with pictures of all the individuals involved, if possible. Or find an item to represent each person.

Lay out a large white cloth (symbolizing peace) and put the pictures/items in the center. Fold in one corner of the cloth at a time, beginning on the northern side, saying,

The cool winds blow to calm anger.

On the west side, saying,

The waves smooth all discord.

On the south side, saying,

The fires are quenched, bitterness cease.

On the east side, saying,

Fresh winds blow with forgiveness and understanding.

Keep the pictures/tokens bound together until the situation resolves.

Increasing Love

For a couple wishing to increase their love, each should take a lock of the other's hair. Holding the lock, recite the name of your loved one three times. Carry the hair as a charm to keep love burning in your heart.

Increasing Love #2

Take some earth where a loved one has stepped and blend it with your hair, nail clippings, and a sprinkling of rose water. Add to a pot in which a flower seed is sown. When the seed sprouts, your love, too, should begin to show signs of growing into maturity.

Increasing Love #3

In Indonesia, lovers wear something belonging to their beloved to increase the love between them. Exchange items during a waxing moon so your love grows to fullness. During the exchange, cooperatively pour warm water on your threshold. This "warms" the way for love each time either of you enters your house.

Decreasing Jealousy

Nothing kills romance faster than the green-eyed monster. To combat this negative energy, attach an image of your partner to one end of a strand of green yarn, preferably a shade you dislike. Snip off sections of the yarn leading to the image, while saying,

> I release jealousy and envy.
> I release mistrust and suspicion.
> I release you.

As you recite the last line of this incantation, snip the yarn away from the image. Burn the yarn so you can't reconnect with any bad energy.

Preserving Love

Find a flower with a magical meaning that expresses your goal. Snip the flower just behind its head, and press it in a favorite love book (maybe a collection of poetry). Whenever you pass the book, or think of it, stop and place both hands on the cover. Visualize white-pink light filling the flower, drying it, and keeping it whole. Say,

> Preserve my love
> as the flower within this book.
> Preserve peace and understanding through all time,
> and keep it with me, fresh in my heart.

Once the flower is dry, leave it in the book to keep love and compassion in the home, or carry it with you to draw positive, long-term love.

Calling Back a Stray Lover

This spell should not be used to force an unwilling partner to return. Instead, it acts as a gentle nudge to bring back someone who has gotten waylaid by circumstances or a rival.

Find a small amount of the herb called dragon's blood. Burn this on wood or paper while repeating the person's name three times. Then say,

> _____ (fill in with name) return to me
> if it be your heart's desire.
> I open the way with this magical fire.
> Hear my voice, but your will remains free.
> Today I pray, you come back to me.

Let the herb burn out in a safe area. Afterward, you may want to call that person and ask to talk over your relationship in a neutral area. If it is meant to be, signs of improvement and deeper commitment will manifest after this meeting.

MAINTAINING LOVE

Adding a spiritual dimension to relationships keeps connections strong, even when your time together is limited. It also fuels the fires of friendship and passion, which are easily neglected. These spells are designed to enhance relationships with a spiritual element.

Remaining Devoted

When you feel temptation beckoning, use love magic to steer your attention back where it belongs. Draw a heart and write the name of your mate in ascending form within it. (This creates a triangle out of the name, with the first letter on top and the full name as the base of the triangle, as in the diagram.) This represents your love growing in body, mind, and spirit.

P
PA
PAU
PAUL

Put your hands, palms down, over the paper and visualize it being filled with pink-white light, while saying,

> *Spirit of creation,*
> *create in me a pure love for* _____
> *(fill in with name).*
> *Let not my mind and heart stray to another*
> *but remain fixed and faithful.*
> *Remind me of my promises, and rekindle our desire*
> *each time I look upon this token. So be it.*

Put the paper where you will see it regularly. If using this magic to improve a job or situation, change the word in the heart to reflect this.

Integrating Change

Relationships that never change will never grow, although the process of change isn't always easy. When you've gone through a harrowing transition in your relationship, this spell will smooth the road ahead.

Place a red candle in a fire-safe container (like a small lantern). Alternatively, use a red flashlight with the light facing the ceiling. From the right to left side of your light source, mark the floor with white tape. The taped line and light mark the boundary between the old way and the beginning of the new.

Stand with your mate, hand-in-hand, on one side of the line. Take turns reciting an incantation such as,

> *The past is behind us,*
> *the future before us.*
> *By crossing this line we mark and accept change.*
> *Using the past as a teacher, not a burden,*
> *looking to the future with hope, not anxiety,*
> *we take the leap of faith*
> *together.*

The last line of this incantation should be recited in unison as you both jump over the line. Blow out the candle and bury the candle (or ritually dispose of the flashlight batteries) to resolve any old tensions or bad feelings. Move forward from this moment with confidence.

Individuals can adapt this spell to integrate personal changes, as well.

Family Feuds

You've heard the old adage, "You can't choose your family." But you can choose to reestablish harmony with them, using magic to smooth the way. This spell can also be used to heal rifts between friends.

Each person needs a white candle and small container of salve. Place a third white candle, the peace candle, between you. Each person lights a candle on the table. In turn, each reaches forward to the central candle and dabs a bit of salve on the wax, saying,

> *Let healing begin.*
> *Where anger dwells, bring forgiveness within.*

Both people then blow out their candles as a sign of truce. This symbolically quells the fire of anger. Sit in the light of the peace candle and talk things out.

Fertility Formula

Fertility magic helps us create the energy necessary to welcome a new life, even if a child is not born to the couple but adopted.

The week before enacting this spell, rest more, eat well, and begin making room and time for a child in your life. Through this week, follow the Italian custom of eating one consecrated apple per day to increase fertility. To bless the apple, say,

> *Great Spirit, bless this fruit*
> *that our union might also be fruitful.*

On the last day of the week, have a quiet, romantic, tender time together. Light a yellow candle near the bed (representing creativity). As you make love, visualize the cresting energy directed toward the woman's womb or any documents associated with an adoption. Let the candle burn completely out, but save the wax.

Soften the wax remnants in a microwave or on the stove and fashion it into the rough likeness of a baby. Swaddle it in warm, white cloth to protect your magic until it manifests.

Forgiveness

A forgiveness spell diffuses anger, using love's energy like an astral salve. It can open the way for healing when one party refuses to speak to the other. You will need something of the other person's (e.g., something that person touched or wore).

In a wooden bowl, mix together sandalwood oil, water, and rose water, stirring counterclockwise and saying,

> *Banish the anger, banish the negativity.*
> *Let my heart and this house be free.*

Stop stirring and focus on your intention to release any lingering bad feelings you may have, then stir clockwise, saying,

> *Let our minds and hearts open.*
> *Let our ears be open.*
> *Replace the pain with receptivity.*
> *_____(individual's name)*
> *please speak with me.*

Visualize this person's face superimposed on the item they touched or wore. Sprinkle the water mixture on it. As this dries, wash your threshold with the remaining water mixture to dispel any negativity and welcome the way for love. Hold the token in your hand when you next contact that person.

Friendship Refresher

Sometimes we forget how important and enriching our friends are. When you wake up and realize this has happened with someone you care about, use love magic to refresh the relationship.

I suggest performing this spell with your friend. Prepare one of the friendship beverages from Chapter 2. Put it into a special serving cup and bless it with a prayer like the following (Fill in the blanks with your friend's name.):

> *In this cup is my gratitude*
> *for the goodness _____'s brought to my life.*
> *May I always appreciate _____*
> *as much as I do today,*
> *and may _____always be blessed.*
> *As we drink from this cup,*
> *let it symbolize our unity and growing love.*

Drink first to internalize the change of perspective and your willingness to accept it. Then let your friend drink from the cup to internalize the blessings placed within it.

Perking Up Passion

Begin with tempestuous music playing in the background and any passion-related incense (see Chapter 3). Light a candle whose color reminds you of intimate moments.

Sit in front of the candle and watch the flame. As it dances and burns, whisper,

> *Fire within; passion within.*
> *Burn, desire within; let my magic begin.*

Keep repeating this phrase and close your eyes, holding the image of the candle's flame in your mind. Visualize the flame growing and slowly moving down through your body, exciting every cell. Continue the visualization until you feel ready to burst. Take that energy and enthusiasm into your lovemaking.

LETTING GO

When love goes awry, or comes to a natural end, it is often hard to let go. This is the purpose of the following spells.

Giving Space

The first step in a separation is to create distance—physical and spiritual. This spell is designed to provide spiritual protection as an emotional bumper, which will also help keep unwanted attentions at bay.

Halfway down the middle of a silver candle, carve a symbol you equate with protection and safety. Before going to bed, light the candle for a few minutes. Use the following incantation, filling in the blank with the name of the person from whom you're separating.

> *Light of silver, like a mirror,*
> *reflect sadness away; only good memories stay.*
> *Between me and _____ put a wall of energy*
> *so both of us might be free.*

As you go to sleep, visualize silver light surrounding you on all sides and extending out like a shield. Repeat this spell each night until the candle has burned out completely.

Breaking It Off

Breaking up involves a lot of mixed feelings. When you are the instigator, use magic to make the transition as positive as possible.

Cut out two paper dolls, connected by their hands, from black paper (to represent banishing). On the night of a waning moon, hold them to the sky, saying,

> *As the moon wanes, so let our feelings fade.*
> *Let my convictions be sure, my heart staid.*
> *Let my words be true but kind.*
> *Between me and _____ all ties unbind.*

As you say the word "unbind," tear apart the paper dolls.

Burn them in separate containers to destroy any negative energy, then meet with that person to end the relationship.

Banishing Unwanted Attention

When someone showers you with undesired affection, to deflect the energy, write the name of the person backwards on a piece of paper and tear it in seven pieces. Burn one piece each night during a waning moon, over seven days. As the paper burns, say,

> *Your attentions avert, your attachment release.*
> *By my will and my words, let your love for me cease!*

Save the ashes from the burnt paper. On the last night bury the ashes at least seven miles away from your residence. If necessary repeat the spell during the next waning moon.

Mending a Broken Heart

The human heart is more fragile than we like to admit. It hurts when people are harsh, critical, grumpy, or inconsiderate. It hurts even more when we've been rejected. At this point it becomes tempting to close our hearts and never risk loving again. But that's not a healthy way to live. Instead, I suggest using magic as a bandage to cover your heart's wound until it heals, then using courage to open up to love again.

You will need a bandage and some lavender oil. Try to work during a waning moon so your sadness "shrinks." Take the bandage in one hand and dab a little lavender oil on the cotton part, saying,

Where pain has been, let healing begin.
Direct to my heart, peace impart.
Let the past fade away, so I can love today.

Wear the bandage over your heart until it falls off by itself. By this time, you should begin feeling better.

Releasing Ties

In a relationship you create astral ties to the other person through exchanged energy. This spell will release those strands so healing can begin for both people.

Find two gray candles and about three feet of gray thread. Tie one end of the thread to one candle and the other end to the second candle. Pull it taut between them. Light both candles, and take a knife or a pair of scissors in hand, saying,

I now release what once was bound.
May healing begin, and peace be found.
Freely detached, your heart and mine,
your mind and mine,
your spirit and mine.

Cut the thread, winding the excess around each candle. Keep one in a safe place (this represents you). Bury the second to represent the emotional and spiritual distance you've placed between yourself and that person.

CHAPTER 5

Love Tokens

"Give me an amulet that keeps intelligence with you. Red when you love, and rosier red, and when you love not, pale and blue."
—R.W. Emerson, *The Amulet*

Nature is filled with objects that can be used in creative ways for magic. Plant parts, such as herbs, flowers, tree parts, roots, fruits, and vegetables, have long been used in forming charms, amulets, and talismans. Stones, crystals, and man-made items like the charms on bracelets, are used similarly.

An amulet is a portable object which has been enchanted for protection. A charm is similar, but instead of repelling energy, it attracts. A fetish is any natural object that represents a higher influence. A talisman is a charm or amulet created at a time of astrological influences corresponding to the magic's goal.

In love magic, charms are the most prevalent, but sometimes other magical objects are more suitable. For example, if you're trying to break off a relationship or repel unwanted attention, an amulet or talisman would be better. The love tokens in this chapter will help you carry your magic wherever you go, inspiring love and romance every day.

Before proceeding, two considerations will help you personalize your tokens:

Color

An object's color is an important element of its power as a love token. You can refer to the associations given in Chapter 2 or, because there are historical variations in color symbolism, I've included these additional meanings here:

Color Associations

Black—establishes foundations; banishing

Blue—calms emotions; peace with self and others

Green—encourages wholeness in a relationship or with self; fertility and luck

Orange—increases personal expressiveness; insight, self-worth, and positive outcomes

Pink—augments attraction; friendship, healing, gentle love, and self-love

Purple—decreases frustration; spiritual love and commitment

Red—enhances sexual enjoyment; assertive and protective love

Yellow—improves community spirit; thoughtful awareness

White—purifies (especially intentions); protective energy

Shape

Certain shapes make us think of specific subjects right away, such as a heart for love. Ancient mages gave metaphysical correspondences to many shapes which have become a part of magical tradition. For example, the circle is considered an integral part of creating sacred space.

Shape Associations

Arrowhead—hitting one's mark; Cupid's arrow

Circle—female fertility; the intimate circles of our lives

Cross, equal-armed—equality and symmetry

Egg—fertility and creativity; new beginnings and healing emotional dis-ease

Heart—energizing all types of love magic

Oblong—male fertility and potency; directing energy (especially if an obelisk)

Square—stability; putting down roots

Star—fulfilling wishes; expanding one's horizons

Triangle—protective energy, especially for one's home and family

Using this information, you could look for a purple, triangular object to safeguard your home and generate spiritual love among family members. Or you could give a round, pink quartz to someone to honor a friendship.

In all instances, the objects should be cleansed before becoming part of your magical efforts. Wash them in salt water, move them through the smoke of a cleansing incense like cedar or pine, or visualize white light pouring into them. This ensures an aurically free, open vessel to absorb and transmit your magical energy.

SEEKING LOVE

Seeking love usually requires that you get out and meet people. This makes portable magical tokens terrific aids in your quest. They create a magical aura around you that communicates your goal to a prospective companion.

Charismatic Aromatic

Scented oils communicate a world of meaning without words. Using a recipe in Chapter 3, or one of your own, prepare a special attraction oil. Pour a little into a small, unbreakable container with three tiny, pink quartz crystals and a small magnet (like those used for refrigerator magnets).

When you go out, dab a little on your pulse points and over your heart, saying,

> Come to me, or me to thee.
> By these words, the magic is freed!

Keep your eyes open, your instincts alert, and see what happens.

Breaking the Ice Charm

The first few minutes of conversation between strangers are usually the hardest. This charm will help you communicate more effectively. Take a large bay leaf and visualize it being filled with golden light. At the same time, use your fingertip to write the word "eloquence" on the leaf, saying,

> *Apollo, god of speech and honesty,*
> *bring to me the words I need,*
> *fill them with confidence, truth, and energy.*

Put the bay leaf in your shoe, pocket, or wallet before leaving the house. If the evening is successful, burn the leaf later, thanking Apollo for his assistance.

Flirtation Fetish

Flirting is part of the dating game. This fetish will make you feel more at ease and frolicsome. Find a small image of a cat. It can be a photograph or drawing, or a small stone or metal figurine. You will also need some dried catnip or valerian, and a white candle.

If possible, create this fetish during the month of April or May, to invoke the Goddess Bast during her traditional festival times. Place the image in a circle formed from the herbs, with the white candle behind it. Just before sunset on the night you plan to go out, light the candle, saying,

> *Goddess of pleasure and fun,*
> *give me assurance and convincing words*
> *before the setting sun.*
> *By the lighting of this candle, my spell is begun.*

Leave the candle to burn safely, and take the image with you to keep Bast's blessing nearby. When you return home, put the image back in its place and leave it there until needed again.

Meeting Potential Friends

An old treatise on amulets says the image of a frog on a beryl stone draws friends to you. Beryl can be found at a rock shop or New Age store. If you can find one carved like a frog, all the better. Otherwise, buy a stone large enough to paint a frog's image on it or use a drawing of a frog wrapped around the stone.

Cleanse overnight in salt water first. Take the stone and the frog image outside when the sun is shining. Imagine the warmth and light of the sun being absorbed by the stone and say,

> Friendship is true, friendship is kind,
> friends this stone will help me to find.
> In the dark, in the light, in or out of my sight,
> by the word "frog" and my will,
> the magic takes flight!

Wrap it with the frog image (or paint the image on it) and take it with you to places where you might meet new friends, such as coffee shops, art galleries, or the zoo. When you are ready, gently touch the stone and whisper the command word "frog." See how many princes and/or princesses show up!

Meeting Potential Friends #2

Sometimes the trick to meeting the "right" people is not to meet the "wrong" ones! This amulet will protect you from those who may not have your best interest at heart. You will need a bloodstone, some camphor oil, and two equal-sized pieces of cloth, one black and one white. If possible, make this during a waning moon for greater banishing power.

Place a few drops of camphor oil on the bloodstone, saying,

> *Those who harm, those who are selfish,*
> *by my will and these words, your interest I banish!*

Wrap the stone with the black cloth, saying,

> *Within this cloth of black is bound*
> *all ill intent, then wrapped around*
> *by a cloth of white, whose purity*
> *when at my side keeps safety with me.*

Wrap the black cloth in the white cloth and tie the bundle together with thread. Carry it with you to keep the wrong people at a distance.

Meeting Potential Mates

An old English tradition instructs that one should place an even-pointed ash leaf, white heather, or a two-leaf clover in the left shoe—items said to draw love to you. The next person you meet will bear an initial of a future mate.

To further empower this token, add an incantation such as:

> *Luck walks with me; love shall I see.*
> *Let my true love come quickly to me!*

After you meet that special someone, remove the token and either preserve it (to safeguard your relationship) or ritually dispose of it with thankfulness.

Meeting Potential Mates #2

A variation on another English tradition is to mix thyme with honey and wine vinegar. Put this blend in an airtight container with a tiny moonstone, saying,

> *Let my eyes be open, let my sight be keen.*
> *Wherever they are, likely mates be seen!*

Keep this mixture with you when you go out, dabbing a bit on your third eye to spiritually "open your eyes" to potential mates. This charm was traditionally considered most potent when performed on St. Luke's Day (October 18).

Glamoury Talisman

This talisman increases your aura of personal attractiveness. It will also improve your ability to give and receive love. You will need a piece of amber that is easily held in your hand. Leave the amber in the light of a full moon for three nights. Each night, put your hands over the stone visualizing the silver light of the moon being absorbed by it and say,

> *Lady moon, fill this stone with your silvery beams.*
> *Whenever it's placed against my body,*
> *let me glow with that same light from within.*

Each time you want to release the magic, rub the amber on your hand or leg while visualizing silver light pouring into your aura. This will create static to spark the magic.

Carving Out Your Wish

Use a small handful of clay, rose water, and a toothpick. Place three drops of rose water on the clay, saying,

> With one, the spell's begun.
> With two, this charm is true.
> With three, bring love to me.

Shape the clay into a heart, and carve the word "love" on it with the toothpick. After the heart dries, carry it with you until your wish manifests.

DEEPENING LOVE

Tucking a little extra magic in your pocket will make moments spent with a companion all the more memorable. These love tokens will enhance quality time and encourage stronger unity.

Commitment Charm

Commitment is really a two-way street, so it's best to make two of these charms so each person can have one.

For two charms you will need three tablespoons of dried orange peel, three sticks of cinnamon, and a sprinkling of cumin. You will also need the petals from two roses, two small woven baskets with tops (these represent two lives "woven" together), and two small pieces of jade. (Inexpensive jade can be found at most New Age stores.)

Mix the orange peel with the cumin, then place half in each basket around the outer edge. Put the rose petals in the middle of the orange peel. Break the cinnamon sticks in half, and fashion triangles from them on top of the rose petals. Then gently put the jade in the center of love's "nest." Bless the containers together, saying,

> *Within this basket woven round*
> *love and devotion, securely bound.*
> *When e'er we carry this stone of jade,*
> *on each other our hearts shall be staid.*

You, your partner, or both of you should carry the jade when your relationship needs some magical bolstering.

Communication Talisman

Find any small, flat, plain rock and some yellow paint or an indelible yellow marker. When the moon is in Aries, paint the rock with the words "speak" and "listen." Carry this with you to make your interactive skills more effective. Hold it for a few moments before going into the situation, visualizing the words as yellow light being absorbed into your mouth. Touch the stone again to reactivate the energy each time you feel yourself fumbling for words.

Attraction Fetish

You will need a turquoise stone and a small length of silver wire. Wrap the stone with the silver, saying,

> *Cupid, take up your bow and arrow,*
> *aim toward this stone; let your mark sure be.*
> *Fill it with love to bring* _____
> *closer to me.*

Fill in the blank with the name of your significant other. Put it in his or her pocket. Afterward, bathe in orange water daily for eight days. If the relationship is meant to deepen, it will show signs by the end of this time.

Pledge Charm

When you and your partner are ready for a deeper commitment, make this charm for each other. Begin with a long strand of white cloth (symbolizing pure intentions) and two equal-sized pieces of cloth from a piece of old clothing. Braid these together, tying the braid at the end.

Take some copper wire (to conduct your energy) and snip off several 4- to 5-inch pieces. Wrap them at equally spaced junctures where all three strands meet on the braid. At each juncture, take turns making one wish for your future together. When this is finished, cut the braid in half so each person can carry one piece. These two halves should be reunited at the wedding or handfasting, then stored in a safe place to ensure continued commitment.

Marriage Charm

Take the rings you intend to exchange and place them on a white candle. Light the candle, visualizing a happy, long-lived relationship and chant,

> *Passionate bliss,*
> *faith and happiness,*
> *love and peace,*
> *let the magic never cease.*

Continue this chant until the candle melts almost to the point of the rings. Remove them and keep the candle to burn on your first anniversary.

MAINTAINING LOVE

No matter where we go, loved ones stay in our hearts and minds. Why not bring our magic with us to keep these relationships strong and fulfilling? These portable tokens will send warm, refreshing energy to those you love, no matter where you go.

Aphrodisiac Fetish

Just before a special meeting with your significant other, place a red rose and a red carnation somewhere on your body. Empower these tokens, saying,

> *Aphrodite, Goddess of Delight,*
> *Within these petals place your power,*
> *bring passion and enchantment this very hour.*

Touch the petals just before seeing your loved one, and repeat the phrase to spark some extra excitement. Dry the petals and keep them as part of an aphrodisiac medicine bag or to burn with incense.

Faithfulness Talisman

An old English spell calls for picking a sprig of knot grass and tying it at the center. Place this close to your heart, saying,

> *Devotion tied within, let the magic now begin.*
> _____ *kept near my heart,*
> *close to me remain, never to part.*

Fill in the blank with the name of your partner. As long as the grass remains tied, devotion will be with you. An alternative for men is to pick a bachelor's button and tie the stem in a knot at its center.

Anti-fascination Amulet

When you feel weakened by the temptations of someone other than your steady, this amulet provides extra willpower. You will need a small carnelian and some scrap of aluminum foil. If possible, create the amulet during a waning moon, so your undesired interest wanes with it.

Take the carnelian in hand and visualize on its surface the face of the person who has been distracting you, until the image is very clear. Wrap the stone with the aluminum, saying,

> *Reflect away, turn my attention back home.*
> *Let my heart not stray, let my eye never roam.*

Carry this token with you when you feel your resolve weakening.

Mystery Glamoury

Mystery and intrigue helps keep interest alive in a relationship. The formula for this type of glamoury depends on whether you want to inspire a man or a woman. For a man, use jasmine or lavender oil; for a woman, use musk oil. Put the oil in a portable vial with a clear quartz point to increase its energy. Leave this in sunlight for three hours for attracting a man; moonlight for attracting a woman.

Carry the vial when you and your partner have a special date planned. Dab on a little before seeing him or her, saying,

> *Magical mystery, empower this glamoury.*
> *To my aura impart a secret art*
> *to please and to tease _____'s heart.*

Fill in the blank with the name of your partner.

Negativity Clearing Amulet

When stress and anxiety begin to interfere with the peaceful-ness of your relationship, try this amulet. Find a jet stone that's easily held in the palm of your hand. Set it under the light of a waning moon for three nights, saying,

> *Tension taken away, negativity drained away,*
> *external influences kept at bay.*

Carry this stone with you for three days, allowing it to absorb all pressures and burdens. On the last day, take it with you in a hot bath. Visualize any remaining tension going down the drain with the water. Be sure to cleanse the stone in salt water afterward if you plan to use it for other purposes.

Banishing Jealousy

When you find yourself becoming possessive of your mate or their time, make this talisman. Find any green stone, a carnelian, and an amethyst, along with a small pouch. Place the stones into the pouch during a dark moon, one at a time, saying,

> *Carnelian decreases jealousy.*
> *Amethyst keeps self-control with me.*
> *This stone of green draws selfishness away.*

Any time your possessive behavior interferes with your relationship, take out one stone and throw it as far as possible, sending those feelings with it. When you need to replace a stone, repeat the incantation to energize the new one.

Enhancing Adoration

To keep devotion and passion alive in your relationship, bind together a sprig each of vervain and St. John's wort in a red cloth, along with a token from your mate. Mark the outside of the cloth with the symbol for Venus, saying,

Red is my love, and deeper still.
The herbs within this cloth of red
keep love and passion in my bed.

Carry this close to your heart so the fire of your relationship continues to burn.

Long-lasting Love Charm

An ancient spell advocates placing three pinches of sand, a feather, and three ground peanuts into a clay pot. Cover this mixture with boiling water and keep it at a slow-rolling boil until the water evaporates (this slowly "warms" and energizes the components). As it boils, strongly visualize your desires in the steam and chant,

Love long as all days,
long as all nights.
Love as lasting as my soul,
let my magic take to flight.

Continue the chant, allowing the volume to grow or diminish as inspiration dictates. Carry the remnants from the pan in a red sachet as a love charm.

LETTING GO

When things go wrong in a relationship, our sadness, confusion, and other negative feelings affect everyone around us. Symbolic tokens of release help decrease that effect and assist us in starting the healing process through positive action.

Reigning in Lust

When you need to keep physical desires under control to help bring a relationship to a healthy ending, use this talisman.

Find a portable item that has a yin-yang symbol on it, such as a ring, earring, or tie tack. Or you can paint one out of gold and silver on a small white cloth. During a waning or dark moon, cup the token in your hands, saying,

> *Dainichi, god of wisdom,*
> *place within this token the sagacity and self-control,*
> *to know and do what is truly best.*
> *Keep my will and intention balanced and sure.*
> *So be it.*

Carry this with you whenever you cross temptation's path.

Turning Away Unwanted Attention

When simply saying "no" isn't enough for a suitor, make this banishing amulet. Write the name of the person backward on a piece of paper. Cut this into seven equal-sized pieces and dab in clove oil. Burn one piece each night for seven nights during a waning moon. As each piece of paper burns, whisper to the smoke,

> *Not to harm, but to heal.*
> *Turn your heart and mind away.*
> *Find another.*

Mix the ashes with bloodstone or onyx, and carry until the problem resolves. At that point, ritually dispose of the ashes in running water, in a fire, or by burial.

Breaking It Off

One of the best amulets for ending a relationship is a blessed, charged piece of fluorite. Besides helping you both to see your situation clearly, the natural 3-D diamond shape of this stone provides a firm foundation on which to base your words.

To charge the fluorite, leave it in sunlight for seven minutes (for a conscious, logical decision) and in moonlight for seven minutes (for sensitivity). Carry this with you, touching it momentarily before delivering the bad news. Afterward, you may want to throw the stone away to detach yourself further from the relationship and its energy.

Healing a Broken Heart

When it seems as if your emotional wounds will never heal, make this token. Take a small, clear amethyst (for self-control), sodalite (for emotional balance), and a carnelian (to decrease anger), and put them in a glass of spring water. Visualize purple, blue-white, and reddish light, respectively, emanating from the stones and filling the water. Take the glass in hand, saying,

> The purple ray to bring balance,
> the blue-white ray to protect and bring peace,
> the red ray, so anger can cease.

Drink the water, then carry the stones with you until you start feeling like your old self again. At that point, you can either ritually dispose of them or purify them for later use.

Forgiveness

One of the most difficult parts of the separation and healing process is forgiveness. Try a talisman made from a clear quartz (to clear energy) and jet (to collect excess negativity). Place the stones in a pouch filled with mint (to inspire peace), along with any object that represents the person you wish to forgive. As you place the token in the pouch, say,

> *Wrapped 'round by peace and good intention,*
> *where anger is stilled, emotions calm,*
> *let this token be a healing balm.*

Carry this with you until you feel forgiveness for that person. Then release the herbs and token to the earth (if biodegradable) and cleanse the stones for other applications.

By keeping our magic with us, it brings more spirituality to everyday situations and helps design our destiny, where love plays an important role. My advice is to let magic shine in love, in life, and in every moment of every day. Single, dating, living together, or married, I guarantee this attitude will change your reality.

CHAPTER 6

Romantic Rituals

"Intimacy becomes a path—an unfolding process of personal and spiritual development."
        —John Welwood

Many beliefs and superstitions around love have remained strong throughout history. Eventually they have filtered into the way we seek out and secure love. Weddings illustrate this filtering process, with superstitions sprinkled throughout their planning and execution (see also Chapter 1).

Enacting a personalized ritual gives you one more active way to help fulfill your love quest. Don't let preconceived ideas of ritual put you off. You already perform rituals every day, by repeating your morning routine, making a meal a specific way, or by taking the same route to work.

In magical traditions, rituals act as prolonged spells, giving more definition and direction to the energy generated. For those seeking additional guidance, I suggest my book, *Wiccan Rituals and Ceremonies, To Ride a Silver Broomstick* by Silver RavenWolf, or *The Spiral Dance* by Starhawk.

Finding the God Within

This ritual reconnects men and women with universal masculine energy. This can help you recognize and empower the god within to increase your leadership ability, strength, and courage. Additionally, this ritual improves your understanding of the men in your life.

Find four god images that you relate to strongly (see Appendix B). Place one in each of the four directions of your sacred space and set up an altar in the center. Place a glass of wine and a red candle on the altar, representing masculinity, fertile fire, and life's blood. Also put an athame (ritual knife) or a wand on the altar as a phallic representation.

Prepare the god incense detailed in Chapter 3, and ignite it in a fireproof container, which you will carry around the circle. Start in the east, holding the burning incense, and recite the following, moving clockwise (fill in the blanks with the names of the god images chosen):

> East— _____,
> *I honor you in my sacred space.*
> *Bring with you the winds of change and power.*
> *Help me hear your voice within myself.*
>
> South—_____,
> *I honor you in my sacred space.*
> *Bring with you the fires of transformation.*
> *Help me see you within myself.*

West—_____,
I honor you in my sacred space.
Bring with you the waters of progress.
Let me feel you within myself.

North—_____,
I honor you in my sacred space.
Bring with you the soils of growth and evolution.
Let me find you within myself.

Next, go to the center of the circle. Put down the incense and light the candle to acknowledge the presence of the divine. Take the wine in one hand and the athame in the other, and close your eyes. Visualize yourself in this circle with each of the god images superimposed over your heart, one at a time. See each image being absorbed into you, feeling its energy and power growing in your heart.

While you work, add a chant such as,

> *The spark of god lies within.*
> *I am divine, I am god.*

Allow the chant to grow louder until it reaches a peak. At that point, dip the athame into your cup (to represent the unity of male and female within you). Remove it and drink half of the wine, then pour the rest out as an offering to the divine beings who lent their assistance to the rite. Spend some time in the sacred space afterward, contemplating the masculine attributes you already have, and those you hope to accentuate.

Close the circle by going to each of the four quarters in reverse order (counterclockwise) and dismissing the sacred energies there. Again, fill in the blanks with the names of the gods represented at those points.

> North—_____ thank you for
> grounding this ritual and empowering me with
> _____ (name an attribute known to
> that god that you wish to integrate).
> Hail and farewell.
>
> West—_____ thank you for helping
> energies to flow within and around this space and
> empowering me with _____.
> Hail and farewell.
>
> South—_____ thank you for your
> power and for kindling the characteristics of
> _____ within me. Hail and farewell.
>
> East—_____ thank you for your fresh
> perspectives and the winds of change. Breathe
> within me, and bring _____ to my
> heart. Hail and farewell.

Blow out the central candle and note any impressions from the ritual in a journal, so you can refer back to it later.

Finding the Goddess Within

This ritual reconnects you with universal feminine energy.

This can help you recognize and empower the goddess within to increase your sensitivity, intuition, and nurturing capacity. Additionally, it will improve your understanding of the women in your life.

Follow the pattern of the first ritual, with the following exceptions: Use goddess images in the four directions and a white candle and wine to represent her presence on the altar; prepare goddess incense from Chapter 3; your ritual cup is a symbol of the womb; change the word "god" in the chant to the word "goddess"; finally, make a list of feminine attributes that you hope to acquire or improve and keep with you during the quiet, meditative time after the libation.

The Call for a Soul Mate

Karmic units form to create specific mini-classrooms for our soul's learning. Within that group, certain souls migrate toward each other again and again, creating strong emotional ties that death can not break. When you meet a person from that karmic unit, something within you recognizes them immediately. The emotional response can be astounding and disturbing. It can easily be mistaken for a meeting with your soul mate. It may be, but that is only one possibility.

I believe the term "soul mate" is a misnomer. To say your soul is tied to one, and only one, other person's soul throughout time sounds very romantic, but it doesn't fit into the ultimate goals of reincarnation: to change, learn, grow, and move on. It seems more likely that several members of your karmic unit have the potential to be life partners, while other people become friends, parents, teachers, and even adversaries. No matter what your views are on this theory, there seems to be a nearly universal desire to seek out that special someone.

The following ritual serves two purposes: It encourages a romantic aura around your life to draw and welcome love; and it gives you peace of mind, knowing you have extended loving energy that will eventually return to you through the right person. It takes time and patience to experience results from this ritual, so repeat it whenever you feel the need. Love is a finicky creature which, like a cat, moves in its own time and manner.

Inscribe a red or pink candle with your name, using a pin or knife. Put it in the sacred space where it will be at eye level when you sit down. Fill a bowl with rose petals and a stick of sandalwood incense.

If possible, perform this ritual outdoors. Take the bowl in hand, and walk clockwise around the sacred space, sprinkling the petals on the ground, saying,

> East—*To the eastern winds I call. Hear my wish. Let these petals reach one with a like mind and soul with whom I can communicate. Bring us together. So mote it be.*

> South—*To the southern winds I call. Hear my wish. Let these petals reach one that I can embrace with passion, and who can return that fervor. Bring us together. So mote it be.*

West—*To the western winds, I call. Hear my wish. Let these petals reach one whose heart is open to give and receive love. Bring us together. So mote it be.*

North—*To the northern winds, I call. Hear my wish. Let these petals reach one with whom a balanced relationship can grow. Bring us together. So mote it be.*

Center—*Light the candle. Spirit, whose light is truth and wholeness, bless this effort. Open the path for love in my life, if it be for the greatest good and harm none. So mote it be.*

Sit comfortably before the candle. Breathe in a slow, rhythmic manner until you feel at ease with your environment. Next, think about someone who makes you feel really loved, allowing these emotions to fill you to overflowing. Direct this loving energy toward your candle (you can visualize this as a pink light pouring out from your heart and enveloping the candle with love and joy). This is an important expression of love to yourself.

Now mentally list the attributes of a good life partner. Be detailed, but try not to limit fate to these restrictions. Formulate a verbal or silent prayer about these characteristics to the divine, and light the incense from the candle's flame. The smoke from the incense carries your prayers to Spirit.

Finally, take a deep breath. As you release it, blow the candle out. Visualize the pink light around the flame being dispersed by your breath in all directions. As you see the energy moving away, whisper your wish for love, and welcome the individual(s) whom this energy will find. Close the ritual by dismissing the quarters while walking clockwise around the sacred space.

> North—*Northern winds, I thank you for your power and for granting levelheadedness on love's quest. Guide my magic safely to its mark as you leave this place.*

> West—*Western winds, I thank you for your power and for granting pure emotions on love's quest. Guide my magic safely to its mark as you leave this place.*

> South—*Southern winds, I thank you for your power and for granting romantic energy to love's quest. Guide my energy to its mark as you leave this place.*

> East—*Eastern winds, I thank you for your power and for granting refreshed hope on love's quest. Guide my energy safely to its mark as you leave this place.*

> Center—*Spirit of creation, I thank you for your*
> *presence and for granting your blessing on my*
> *magic. Guide my spell and my path until love's*
> *quest is fulfilled. Farewell.*

In a journal make notes of your experience, and any ways in which you personalized the ritual, for future reference. Keep the candle and repeat the rite when you feel the need. Carry some of the melted wax with you as a love-drawing charm until the magic manifests.

Releasing Expectations

Every generation has different concepts of the perfect relationship. Until recently, it was common to see relationships portrayed in the media as blissfully happy, with love as the binding tie that conquered anything. And while contemporary portraits are somewhat more realistic, many depictions are still idealistic.

Relationships can be happy and strong, but are difficult to achieve if one or both partners assumes that love will conquer all. Love is but one ingredient in a very complex recipe. The others include trust, communication, respect, perseverance, tolerance, and a heaping spoonful of patience.

There is no such thing as a flawless mate or relationship, and our magical expectations should reflect this. By accepting others—and ourselves—as we are, we can move forward on even footing.

For this ritual you will need a small doll to represent each person participating in the exercise, 12 strands of yarn or ribbon tied to each doll, a pair of scissors for each person, a white candle to represent truth and pure intentions, and a container to burn the ribbons in.

If possible, the job of calling the quarters should be shared, one person invoking the east and south, another invoking the west and north.

> East—*Winds of wisdom, insight, and change,*
> *come bless us with your breath*
> *and help manifest our magic.*
>
> South—*Fires of energy and perfect love,*
> *come bless us with your warmth*
> *and help empower our magic.*
>
> West—*Waters of healing and peace,*
> *come bless us with your gentle truth*
> *and help our magic to flow.*
>
> North—*Soils of foundation and growth,*
> *come bless us with your security*
> *and help our magic mature.*
>
> Center—Light the white candle and say together, *Only the light of truth and love shall shine here.*

This enacts a promise that you will be honest and compassionate with one another in the sight of the Sacred. Remember, this isn't a time to complain about negative habits, but to release each other from unhealthy expectations which hinder your relationship's growth.

Next, each person in turn cuts one ribbon off the other's doll, verbally acknowledging a released expectation. For example, if a friend, partner, or mate tends to be tardy, you might say, "I release you from my personal concept of timeliness." Another fitting application for this ritual is releasing each other from outward imperfections, such as being overweight. Focusing on the external takes away from spiritual connections, especially in long-term, intimate relationships. You could use a positive phrase instead, such as, "I love you the way you are." By releasing your criticism of the loved one, you are actually reinforcing (on a subconscious level) a healthy alternative and decreasing tension tremendously.

Continue this exercise until all the ribbons have been cut. This disconnects all the expectation "tethers." Ignite the ribbons in the candle's flame and let them burn so you can't reattach them. Keep the freed image of your loved one where you can see it regularly, as a reminder of your promises.

This exercise can also be used to release yourself from unreasonable goals, ideals, and so on.

Forgiveness

We all make mistakes. When those mistakes hurt someone close to us, an apology helps, and a ritual also promotes emotional healing. Each person should find a disposable symbol of their anger. Gather two red candles, one white candle, a twenty-one-inch length of white ribbon, and lavender incense.

If you use an athame in your magic, use extra white ribbon to "peace bond" the blade (tie it so it can't come out of the sheath). This represents your desires to maintain a truce and work toward harmony. I also suggest sharing the responsibility for calling the quarters, since forgiveness and accord require mutual effort.

Put the ribbon and white candle on a central table or altar, unlit. Light the lavender incense. Carry your personal red candles (lit) while calling the quarters. Begin in the north and move counterclockwise (to banish anger).

> North—*Concordia, goddess of peace and harmony,*
> *quell the anger in our hearts, and replace it with*
> *renewed understanding and love so healing can begin.*

> West—*Aleitheia, goddess of truth, bless this sacred*
> *space with honest, gentle words so healing may begin.*

> South—*Anu, god of fairness and mediation,*
> *come and oversee our rite. Let us both accept our*
> *responsibility to this relationship, its sorrows and*
> *joys, so healing can begin.*

> East—*Forseti, god of justice, let your fairness and balance be our guide in this sacred space so healing can begin. So be it.*

Take your individual candles and place them to each side of the white one. Take your partner's hand, look into his or her eyes and say "I'm sorry." In unison, light the central white candle with the red ones saying, "We accept forgiveness and peace into our hearts." Blow out the candles of anger and bind them tightly with the white ribbon. Spend time in the sacred space talking things out calmly.

When you're ready, dismiss the quarters, moving clockwise to maintain the positive energy you've created.

> East—*Forseti, thank you for blessing this time with balanced judgment and equity. Go in peace, and keep peace between us.*

> South—*Anu, thank you for helping us negotiate, using love as a guide. Go in peace, and keep peace between us.*

> West—*Aleitheia, thank you for the honesty necessary to put our relationship back on track. Go in peace, and keep peace between us.*

> North—*Concordia, thank you for the harmony established in this sacred space this day. Go now in peace, and keep peace between us. Farewell.*

After the ritual, put away the anger candles in a safe spot where you can find them again, if needed. Light the peace candle daily until it burns out completely to remind you of your mutual commitment.

Healing a Broken Heart

Unlike the reed, which is able to bend in every wind, the human heart finds it hard to accept difficult changes in a relationship. You can help integrate change and begin healing through ritual.

This ritual requires a poppet (a small cloth figurine) filled with lavender (for peace), dried apple peel (for emotional health), pine needles (for cleansing negativity), and a carnelian (for renewed self-confidence). The poppet represents you, so, if possible, fashion it from a piece of personal clothing and dab it with a bit of your perfume.

Take this into your sacred space along with a white candle, a cup of dry (not sweet) wine, and seven sticks of violet incense (to promote self-love). Call the quarters, saying,

> East—*Winds of change, move away my pain; teach me to free what cannot be grasped. Cool my anger, my frustration. Refresh my soul; make me whole.*

> South—*Fires of cleansing, burn away my sadness; teach me to release what cannot be held. Energize my faith, my self-confidence. Burn anew in my soul; make me whole.*

West—Waters of healing, wash away my
wounds; teach me to flow with what cannot be
stopped. Cleanse me with tears. Crest with hope in
my soul; make me whole.

North—Earth of foundations, re-root me in your
soil; teach me to stand so I cannot be shaken.
Ground me in reality, in conscious awareness.
Revitalize my soul; make me whole.

Light a stick of incense from the flame of the white candle
and set it aside. Take the cup in hand, saying,

Timeless, wise Spirit. I have tasted bitter sadness
recently (sip from the cup and dab some wine on the
poppet's heart) but the time for sorrow is past.
I release it to you and the earth, and ask for joy
in its place.

Pour the remnants of the cup out as a libation to the earth.
If you can't do this in the sacred space, do so outside afterward.

Put your hands over the doll, visualizing it filled with pink-
white light until it overflows with energy. As you do so, chant,
As to thee, so to me; let love begin within.

Leave the doll in the path of the smoke until the incense
burns out. Use this time to cry, laugh, dance, or whatever it
takes to release your pain.

Close the circle, beginning in the north, saying,

North—*Mother, hold me close to your breast until I meet with you again. Thank you for being here to help my heart mend.*

West—*Sister, let me sleep on waves of comforting until I meet with you again. Thank you for being here to help my heart mend.*

South—*Father, let my spirit ignite again with hope until I meet with you again. Thank you for being here to help my heart mend.*

East—*Brother, let my soul rejoice in your whimsical winds until I meet with you again. Thank you for being here to help my heart mend. Hail and farewell.*

For the next week, burn a stick of the violet incense before you go to bed, and repeat, *As to thee, so to me; let love begin within.*

Hold the doll close to you while you sleep to extend love to yourself. Ritually burn or bury the doll when you feel whole again.

Engagement

An engagement ritual symbolizes the promise and pledge of love without the legally binding paperwork. Afterward, the couple has time to review their relationship seriously, and make or break future plans. I feel an engagement ritual should be entered into with as much sobriety as a marriage.

Perform this ritual in the light of a waxing moon, to emphasize growth of the relationship. For an engagement empowered by magic, each person should choose a token to give to the other. Have a cup of water, two lit candles, and two unlit candles on an altar central to the sacred space. Each person should take turns calling the quarters to emphasize equality. Recite the invocation to Spirit together.

> East—*In the place of a rising sun, we make our pledge to each other and the ancients. Let a fresh wind wrap round us with conscious awareness of what our promises mean.*

> South—*In the place of a noonday sun, we make our pledge to each other and the ancients. Let a warm fire wrap round us with constant love and passion to kindle the longevity of our promise.*

> West—*In the place of a setting sun, we make our pledge to each other and the ancients. Let waves of emotion wrap round us, keeping our promise fresh and full.*

> North—*In the place of a dark sun, we make our pledge to each other and the ancients. Let rich soil provide ground within which our promise shall grow to fullness.*

> Spirit—*In the place beyond space and time, we make our pledge to each other and the ancients. Let*

> Spirit and the ancients witness our promise, and
> bless it with their presence.

Stand together before the altar. Each person, in turn, should take one of the lit candles and ignite one of the unlit ones, saying,

> This flame was my being before I met you. Today I
> become someone new because of our promise to each
> other. Today I accept a place in your heart, like a
> seed that will grow into the tomorrows.

Extinguish the flame of the first candle in the cup in turn, saying,

> The past is behind me. It has shaped me and what I
> have become, but it does not restrict the possibilities
> our love gives to the future. Let any bad memories die
> here today, and let devotion be born with our pledge.

Turn to one another and place the palm of your strong hand over your partner's heart, saying in turn,

> I am part of your heart, and you are part of mine.
> Today I pledge my love to you so that over the next
> _____ (number of weeks, months, or years until
> the wedding) we can grow in unity toward what-
> ever the future holds. Do you accept my pledge?

Each partner replies, adding anything they feel they need to say. Then give the tokens you've brought, explaining their significance. These tokens should be carried as often as possible, as charms to inspire your love and strengthen your pledges.

Close the circle, beginning in the north, saying,

> North—*Powers of the north, we thank you for your presence and blessing. Your sky, dark as the soil, but filled with stars, represents our hearts filled with hope and possibilities.*

> West—*Powers of the west, we thank you for your presence and blessing. Your waters, blue as the sky, and brimming with life, represent our desire to flow with one another into the future.*

> South—*Powers of the south, we thank you for your presence and blessing. Your fires, red as the sun, and filled with energy, represent our passion and warmth.*

> East—*Powers of the east, we thank you for your presence and blessing. Your winds, invisible as breath, yet as vital, represent our love which cannot be seen, but is known deep within.*

To close the ritual, I suggest writing and reciting a prayer together that expresses your feelings at this moment.

Marriage or Handfasting

The magic of unity comes from ritual marriage, the blessings of the divine and of kin. A marriage or handfasting celebrates everything about love, and all its possibilities.

Marriage is a very personal observance. Both people's culture, spiritual beliefs, tastes, and families figure heavily into the creation of the ceremony. I've provided an outline here specifically for a couple whose magical path is known to their guests. This outline offers ideas, not edicts. Fill out the rest by following your heart and vision.

Begin by decorating the sacred space to reflect the occasion. Knot magic neatly ties the wishes for your relationship into each bow. Bells announce the union to others and chase away evil influences. Anything white or silver symbolizes purity and the presence of Spirit to bless the gathering. Add significant flowers (see Appendix A), aromatics, and anything else that feels right. Put colored balloons, candles, or other tokens at the four quarter points to prepare the sacred space.

Calling the quarters depends on the couple's spiritual path. Consider invoking gods and goddesses from your personal pantheon to witness and bless the rite, or use an invocation that everyone present will understand. Some couples have a priest or priestess invoke the guardians before the guests arrive if family members are uncomfortable with magic.

Once inside the sacred space, the ritual can be as diverse and unique as the couple. Some magical traditions you might want to use are:

- Drinking from one cup to symbolize your united destiny. This was an ancient pagan and gypsy custom.

- Lighting a central candle together to represent the sacred energy that binds two people in love.

- Binding your hands together with cloth or flowers representing oneness and accord. This is how the word "hand-fasting" originated.

- Jumping over a broom handle or sword blade to mark your transition into a new life together. This also brings figurative or literal fertility, depending on the couple's wishes.

After the ritual, gift exchanges, toasts, cake cutting, and showers of confetti are all common, and have vestiges of magic within them. In earlier times, the people gave symbolic gifts such as bread so that the couple would never want for food. Toasts were originally a type of invocation and offering to the divine. Cakes began in Rome where they were crumbled over the heads of the couple and eaten for fertility, abundance, and providence. Lastly, as the couple leaves the celebration, a shower of rice or bread crumbs ensures prosperity and fertility and inspires a "shower" of blessings.

Separation

When a marriage or long-term relationship doesn't work out, it takes a lot of effort to keep the separation process peaceful and constructive. By enacting a mutually agreed upon rite, you can release each other and possibly maintain a friendship.

You need scissors, a fire source like a brazier or small cauldron, a small amount of salve, and a photograph of the two of you together. Each should take turns calling the quarters. It took two people to make this relationship and it will take two to disperse that energy. Begin in the north as a symbol of termination.

North—*Ancient Powers of the Earth, hear us all;*
Hearken to our urgent call.
Help us weather the storm in our hearts.
Help us to heal as we part.

West—*Ancient Powers of the Water, hear us all;*
Hearken to our urgent call.
Help us ride the wave of shifting tides.
While we part, stand by our sides.

South—*Ancient Powers of the Fire, hear us all;*
Hearken to our urgent call.
Help us govern the flames of wrath.
Help us walk a peaceful path.

East—*Ancient Powers of the Air, hear us all;*
Hearken to our urgent call.
Help us abide the winds of change.
Help us forgive, and our lives rearrange.

Go together before the altar. One person should hold the photograph while the other cuts it halfway apart, separating your two images. Then switch, cutting the photo completely in half. Now take the image of your partner and dab a little salve on it, saying,

> *I wish you wellness and wholeness, and release you*
> *without malice. While our intimacy wanes, may*
> *friendship remain.*

Burn the images to complete the release process and send your prayers to the divine. Share with each other any parting thoughts you may have, then close the circle starting in the east (to mark a new beginning), and moving clockwise to keep positive energy with both of you.

> East—*Powers of the east, thank you for attending*
> *this rite. Help us move from this place in peace with*
> *renewed confidence as our guide.*

> South—*Powers of the south, thank you for*
> *attending this rite. Help us move from this place*
> *cleansed of anger, with light as our guide.*

> West—*Powers of the west, thank you for attend-*
> *ing this rite. Help us move from this place in whole-*
> *ness, with forgiveness as our guide.*

> North—*Powers of the north, thank you for*
> *attending this rite. Help us move from this place*
> *founded in love, with hope as our guide.*

If possible, leave the sacred space by two separate exits.

Rededication (Vow Renewal)

After being married for well over a decade now, I understand and respect the value of rededication. There are times when two people drift apart, when circumstances pressure the joy right out of a relationship, or when we forget just how precious it is. Rededication brings refreshment and renewed appreciation of our partner.

Rededication is as personal as marriage, perhaps even more intimate. Many people use elements from their marriage or handfasting rite for this ritual, but do not necessarily invite guests. Other people can support the magic through communal love and blessing, while enacting the ritual alone allows for more uninhibited tenderness.

As with the marriage ritual, I'm presenting only an outline, leaving many details up to you. Decorations should reflect your relationship and its growth. Bring pictures of major moments in your lives and special gifts given to each other. Wear each other's favorite outfit and scent. Make a list of the things you love about each other.

Call the quarters according to your personal tradition. Keep the atmosphere as cozy as possible, possibly with candlelight or a roaring fire. Spend time with the ancients and each other, recalling the reasons you came together in the first place.

When the time seems right, recite your vows again, or any new promises beneath the gaze of the Sacred. At the end of the ritual, spend the rest of the day or night together reminiscing and rejoicing.

Rituals are important, but how you express, give, and receive love every day carries even more power. Without the daily practice of love, spells and rituals, charms and chants amount to nothing more than going through the motions. Love must come through consistent word and deed. This consistency and dedication is part of spirituality, and it is the fuel that will spark your magic to miraculous results.

Love well!

APPENDIX A

Ingredients for Love

This book includes spells, charms, and glamouries for bringing love into your life. However, magic is often more meaningful and successful when created from scratch. This appendix provides you with potential ingredients for those recipes.

Using the spells and tokens described in this book as a starting point, substitute different components, words, and timing to suit your goals. Also consider reading my book *Spinning Spells, Weaving Wonders* for a more in-depth guide to spellcraft.

I listed only components and associations specifically related to relationship and love magic. Many of these components also have other metaphysical correspondences not given here.

Component	Magical Association
Acorn	Increases masculine sexual prowess
Agate	Inspires amiable agreements and truthfulness
Agate (black)	Represents spiritual love
Amber	Inspires beauty, the ability to give and receive love, and sensuality

Amethyst	Generates improved self-control. Eases heartache. Stimulates good judgment, hope, and emotional love. Attracts women.
Apple	Encourages a healthy, responsible love
Aquamarine	Helps with keeping a cool head
Beech (leaf or nut)	Improves physical endurance
Beryl	Prevents fascination and increases friendly feelings. Attracts love.
Betel nut	Encourages a relationship that leads to marriage
Bloodstone	Decreases unwanted interest
Bread	Accents the spirit of sharing and kinship
Briony	Adds power to love potions
Camphor	Repels unwanted lovers
Caraway	Stabilizes devotion
Carnation	Inspires interest from others
Carnelian	Decreases jealousy and anger. Improves confidence. Stimulates sexual interest.
Cherry blossom	Brings luck to love
Chrysanthemum	Brings contentment

Colors:

Black	Banishes unwanted attention
Blue	Inspires joy and contentment
Brown	Secures foundations
Green	Inspires growth

Gray	Restores balance
Orange	Attracts warm feelings and friends
Purple	Evokes spiritual love and kinship
Red	Energizes passionate love
White	Engenders protection and peace
Yellow	Stimulates creativity and fertility
Copper	Stimulates and conducts energy
Cucumber	Increases fertility
Cupid	Arouses emotion
Date	Improves male fertility and sexual prowess
Diamond	Represents eternal love
Doves	Epitomize gentle love and fidelity
Egg	Accentuates fertility and gradual progress
Fig	Arouses erotic love
Fish	Improves fertility
Flame	Energizes passionate, physical love
Flower petals	Release your wishes to the winds
Flowers	Inspire blossoming feelings
Fluorite	Clarifies perception
Forget-me-nots	Symbolize yearning
Gardenia	Augments attractiveness
Garlic	Encourages physical prowess that can result in many children
Garnet	Emphasizes passion, affection, and friendship
Ginseng	Improves virility

Gold	Encourages a long-lasting love
Hands, clasped	Encourages agreement and accord
Hearts	Represent romantic love
Hematite	Helps in developing friendship
Holly	Increases joy
Honey	Inspires gentle love and compassion
Honeysuckle	Generates generous love
Hoopoe	Brings love's message to you or another
Iron	Blocks enchantments, especially charms
Jade	Represents eternal love and commitment
Jasmine	Attracts joyful love
Jasper	Increases beauty
Jasper, red	Attracts passionate lovers
Lapis	Motivates fertility, devotion, and spiritual love
Lavender	Encourages peaceful relationships
Lemon	Represents matters of the heart and pure intentions
Lettuce	Acts as an aphrodisiac
Locket	Secures friendship and devotion
Lodestone	Attracts wanted attention
Lovage	Attracts attention
Magnolia	Represents the offer of a favor
Meadow lily	Secures adoration
Mistletoe	Promotes "kissability"

Moon:

Waxing moon	Encourages growth in relationships
Full moon	Represents maturity in relationships
Waning moon	Helps with separation or banishing
Dark moon	Encourages healing or a "time out"

Moonstone	Highlights tender love and gentle protection
Mother of pearl	Focuses on fertility
Mulberry	Provokes wisdom
Musk	Arouses sexual excitement
Myrtle	Depicts happiness
Narcissus	Banishes vanity
Olive	Encourages reconciliation
Onyx	Decreases or balances sexual desire
Orange	Increases devotion, faithfulness, and fertility
Oyster	Improves fertility
Pansy	Acts as a love charm
Patchouli	Helps with feeling attractive and sexy
Pearl	Represents purity of intent
Perfume	Amplifies personal energy and charisma
Pineapple	Energizes hospitality, welcome, and fertility
Pine cone	Enhances male sexuality
Plum	Enhances female sexuality
Plum blossom	Symbolizes innocent love
Pomegranate	Engenders fertility
Poppy	Engenders fertility

Quartz (clear)	Increases or stores energy
Quartz (pink)	Stimulates friendship, affection, and fidelity
Reed	Inspires flexibility
Ring	Represents eternity
Rock (plain)	Establishes firm foundations and durability
Rose	Enlivens courtship, beauty, and marriage
Ruby	Improves passion and deepens love
Salt	Cleanses negative emotions
Sandalwood	Clears anger
Seeds	Begin a cycle of growth
Silver	Inspires love, peace, and protective energy
Snake	Improves male fertility
Sodalite	Inspires emotional balance and wisdom
Spider	Evokes one's fate or destiny
Starfish	Symbolizes the undying power of love
Succulents	Aid with abundant love
Swan feather	Demonstrates faithfulness and fidelity
Tiger's eye	Accentuates confidence and warm feelings
Topaz	Warms relationships
Tulip	Improves love
Turquoise	Fulfills friendship
Venus (planet)	Represents all matters of love
Water	Circulates emotions; cleanses

Weekdays:

Monday	Focuses on hearth, home, self-love, and intuition
Tuesday	Focuses on passion, physical expression, assertive love, and pleasure
Wednesday	Focuses on communication
Thursday	Focuses on fun and adventure
Friday	Focuses on devotion and commitment
Saturday	Focuses on practicality and socialization
Sunday	Focuses on friendship, blessing, and rejuvenation

Wheat sheath	Improves abundance and fertility
Willow	Accentuates beauty, grace, and flexibility

Winds:

North	Gives foundation to a relationship
East	Provides new beginnings or clean breaks
South	Energizes passion and romance
West	Augments emotional issues, "going with the flow"

Yew	Dispels love charms

Gods, Goddesses, Heroes, and Heroines of Love

The world's myths, legends, and histories are filled with hundreds of illustrations of good friends, companions, life mates, and lovers. Some teach us valuable lessons through powerful symbolism. These are the archetypes of love to call on for positive change in our relationships.

By focusing on a specific facet of the god/dess or other historical persona, you draw that energy into your magical goals. Calling on Venus, for example, or using her image on your altar or as part of a visualization, is quite appropriate for sensual and romantic love.

Adonis (Greek)	God of physical beauty
Aengus (Irish)	God of youthful love
Agassou (Haitian)	God of custom and tradition
Agni (Hindu)	God of beneficence and fertility; honor him with hibiscus in the sacred space
Ahsonnutl (Navajo)	God of bisexuality

Aitvaras (Lithuanian)	House guardian who can be appeased with eggs
Aladdin (Arabian)	Hero who overcame the odds of a love hindered by social constraints and powerful enemies
Aleitheia (Gnostic)	Goddess of truthfulness; honor her with any paired items in the sacred space
Ama No Uzume (Japanese)	Goddess of erotic dance, attraction, and fertility
Anagke (Greek)	Goddess of destiny and necessity
Anaitita (Persian)	Goddess of marriage and childbirth who specifically cares for women; invoke her on the tenth day after a new moon
Anat (Canaanite)	Goddess of love and fertility, thought to be God's mistress; her symbols are the lion and bear
Anu (Assyro-Babylonian)	God of arbitration
Aphrodite (Greek)	Goddess of sex and passion; invoke her on April 23 or June 24 with rose incense, or an offering of copper and turquoise
Apollo (Greek/Roman)	God of fertility, truth, and eloquence; honor him with bay leaves
Aramati (Hindu)	Goddess of devotion and fidelity

Arani (Hindu)	Goddess of sexual fire and alternative lifestyles
Arthur (European, Celtic)	Hero of forgiving and forbearing love
Astarte (Canaanite)	Goddess of fertility; invoke her on April 23, or any Friday or Saturday
Atergatis (Syrian)	Goddess of fertility and wisdom whose sacred animals are the fish and snake
Baccus (Roman)	God of playfulness, fertility, wine and celebration; honor him with musk incense
Baldur (Scandinavian)	God of wisdom and goodness
Bast (Egyptian)	Goddess of playfulness, joy, sex, and physical pleasure
Belit-Ilanit (Chaldean)	Goddess of eroticism, peace, and kindness; she brings people together
Benten (Japanese)	Goddess of luck, love, and communication
Bullai-Bullai (Aborigine)	Goddess of star-crossed lovers
Cecrops (Roman)	Hero who instituted marriages and established communities
Cinderella (Fictional)	Heroine of seemingly impossible relationships and karmic reprisal
Cleopatra (Egyptian)	Heroine of women who wish to be more desirable

Concordia (Roman)	Goddess of peace and harmony; invoke her on January 16, January 20, March 30, April 1, or June 11
Cupid (Roman)	God of love, son of Venus; his symbol is a bow and arrow
Da-bug (Slavonic)	God of hearth and home
Dahud (Breton)	Goddess of uninhibited allure
Dainichi (Japanese)	God of pure intention and wisdom
Delight (Hindu)	Goddess of desire, joy, and beauty
Deus Fidius (Roman)	God of hospitality and welcome
Devi (Indian, Chinese)	Goddess of pure intentions and creative, loving exchanges
Diarmaid (Irish)	Hero of lovers who love despite the odds
Dionysus (Greek)	God of fertility and ecstasy; honor him with an offering of wine
Eos (Greek)	Goddess of desire, fresh beginnings, and youthful love
Eros (Greek)	God of love and relationships; son of Aphrodite
Erzulie (Haitian Voodoo)	Goddess of love and lovers who make things as they ought to be; her color is blue
Fand (Irish)	Goddess of pleasure and lovers
Fides (Roman)	Goddess of fidelity and honorable intentions

Forseti (Scandinavian)	God of justice and peace
Fortuna (Roman)	Goddess of luck and fate; her emblem is a turning wheel
Freyja (Teutonic)	Goddess and protectress of marriage
Fudo-myoo (Japanese)	God of wisdom, kindness, and mercy
Fuh Sing (Chinese)	God of happiness; his symbol is a bat
Ganesa (Hindu)	God of luck, wisdom, and joy; honor him with jasmine incense
Guenevere (French)	Heroine of friends who become lovers
Harmonia (Greek)	Goddess of peace, harmony, love, and charm
Hastsehogan (Navajo)	God of the home
Hawthor (Egyptian)	Goddess of beauty and uninhibited sexuality; invoke her on September 17 or October 16 with sandalwood and rose incense
Hera (Greek) *(called Juno in Rome)*	Goddess of ideal relationships; honor her with myrrh incense
Hermes (Greek)	God of communication; honor him with sandalwood incense and agate stones
Hestia (Greek)	Goddess of the home
Hotei (Japanese)	God of laughter and happiness; his symbol is a linen pouch or sack

Hulda (Teutonic)	Goddess of marriage and fecundity
Inanna (Sumerian)	Goddess of sacred marriage; invoke her on New Year's Day
Indrani (Hindu)	Goddess of attraction and pleasure
Isani (Hindu)	Goddess of blessings and fertility
Isolde (French)	Heroine who reminds us of the responsibility that goes with love magic
Kama (Hindu)	God of love, much like Cupid and Eros, bearing a bow and arrow
Kannon Bosatu (Japanese)	God of compassion
Kara (Teutonic)	Goddess of charm
Kichijo-ten (Japanese)	Goddess of beauty and good fortune
Krishna (Hindu)	Represents divine love, fidelity, and the desire to reunite with Spirit
Kwan Yin (Chinese)	Goddess of fecundity and compassion who hears the cries of people's hearts
Lakshmi (Hindu)	Goddess of beauty, radiance, and fortune; honor her with a willow branch
Lasya (Tibetan)	Goddess of beauty; her symbol is a mirror
Liban (Irish)	Goddess of joy and pleasure
Lono (Polynesian)	God of fertility; honor him with a libation of salt water

Marc Anthony (Roman)	Hero of strong, passionate men
Meni (Chaldean)	Goddess of love and fate
Min (Egyptian)	God of sexual potency; honor him with fresh flowers
Nanan-Bouclou (Benin)	God of bisexuality; honor him with fresh herbs
Narcissus (Greek)	Mythological archetype for self-love that becomes egotistical
Neith (Egyptian)	Goddess of marriage and domesticity; invoke her on June 24
Netzach (Hebrew)	Goddess of emotions
Nunakawa-Hime (Japan)	Goddess of diplomacy in relationships; she gives us wisdom
Ogun (Nigerian)	God of lovers; his symbol is fire
Omactl (Aztec)	God of joy and celebration
Oshun (Nigerian)	Goddess of beauty, lavish dress, and pleasingly scented oils, lotions, and powders
Perchta (Slavonic)	Goddess of fertility and beauty
Priapus (Greek)	God of phallism and fertility; invoke his presence with musk incense
Prometheus (Greek)	God of wise advice; champion of humankind's needs
Pushan (Hindu)	God of relationships and marriage
Rakshasis (Hindu)	Goddess of bewitchment and charm

Rangi (Maori)	God of embraces and creation
Rati (Hindu)	Goddess of sexual pleasure and passion
Ruth (Hebrew)	Biblical heroine of devoted friendship
Samkhat (Babylonian)	Goddess of joy
Sati (Egyptian)	Goddess of love and fertility; her symbol is antelope horns
Semo Sanctus (Roman)	God of oaths and promises
Shala (Chaldean)	Goddess of kindness and compassion
Silenus (Greek)	God of joy, wisdom, and insight
Sjofna (Teutonic)	Goddess of love in all forms
Sodasi (Hindu)	Goddess of all things complete, perfect, and beautiful; her symbol is the lotus
Sradda (Hindu)	Goddess of confidence and trust
Tara (Tibetan)	Goddess of eroticism, love, and compassion; her symbols include a lion and a lotus
Tellus Mater (Roman)	Goddess of fecundity; invoke her on April 15
Tian Kuan (Chinese)	God of happiness, well-being, and family
Tlazolteotl (Aztec)	Goddess of beauty, love, fertility, and magic; honor her with a bowl of rich soil

Tristan (Celtic)	Hero of lovers who face tremendous difficulties
Turan (Etruscan)	Goddess of love, passion, and fertility; similar to Venus
Tvashtar (Hindu)	God of excitement
Vesta (Roman)	Goddess of all domestic matters; honor her with any type of fire
Xochipilli (Aztec)	God of love, lovers, and marriage; invoke him during the seventh hour of the day
Yarilo (Slavonic)	God of passion, sexual love, and fertility; honor him with fresh flowers and erotic dancing

Love's Holidays and Festivals

People celebrate the spirit of friendship, love, and romance all over the world. St. Valentine's Day, for example, originated in ancient Rome as a celebration called Lupercalia with very sensual overtones. Today, Valentine's Day is a time for unbridled romance, rich in symbolic tradition. Lacy cards capture the attention of a desired one, knots bind love into packages, candies make a relationship sweet, and roses inspire or speak of adoration.

This appendix lists other love-centered holidays and their themes. If you're looking for a day to emphasize and support the magic in an amulet, spell, or ritual, there is probably one here suitable to your goal.

January 1 *Gamelia Day (Greece)*	Marriage. Getting married today brings especially good fortune to the couple
January 3 *Inanna's Day (Sumeria)*	Transcendent love that overcomes all odds

January 11 *Carmentalia (Rome)*	Fertility, especially for women; a good time to bless children
January 20 *Festival of the Kitchen God (China)*	Family unity and ethics
January 21 *St. Agnes' Day (Europe)*	Dreaming of one's future love(s)
January 28 *St. Charlemagne Day (France)*	Appreciating wise, supportive in-laws and/or parents
January 30 *Festival of Pax (Rome)*	Peace; putting the past behind you to bring blessings
February 4 *Bean Throwing Day (Japan)*	Bringing luck to one's home and family
February 14 *St. Valentine's Day (Rome)*	See above
February 18 *Parentalia (Rome)*	Honoring one's family and ancestors
February 22 *Concordia's Day (Rome)*	Harmony among people
February 23 *Terminalia (Rome)*	Protecting one's home, property, and loved ones

February 26 *Festival of Mihr (Armenia)*	Bringing prosperity to one's home and accentuating beauty
February 29 *Leap Year Day (Various)*	Playful love; an opportunity to ask out someone you are attracted to
March 2 *Feast of Vesta (Rome)*	Hearth and home; keeping a fire or lamp burning all day to emphasize unity and love in your living space
March 9 *Festival of Aphrodite and Adonis (Greek)*	Celebrating love with one's lover
March 11 *Feast of Gauri (India)*	Giving thanks for one's mate
April 1 *Veneralia (Rome)*	Sexuality, specifically taking pleasure in one's body
April 5 *Kwan Yin Day (Japan)*	Marriage, the home, and children
May 1 *May Day (England)*	Fertility; weaving magic to change your social fate
May 5 *Festival of Banners (Japan)*	Accentuating traditional male qualities
May 18 *Feast of Pan (Greek)*	Male sexuality

May 21 *Festival of Savitri (Hindu)*	Fidelity
May 25 *Celebration of Tao (China)*	Harmony within and with other people
June 4 *Festival of Roses (Greek)*	Romance and passion
June 17 *Marriage of Orpheus* *and Eurydice (Greek)*	Unity; spending time with one you love
June 24 *Luck Day (Europe)*	Improving fortune
June 25 *Midsummer's Day (Various)*	Performing spells and divinations for improving or discovering love
July 7 *Tanabata (Japan)*	Bringing success to seemingly hopeless love, or bringing distant loves closer
August 9 *Feast of the* *Milky Way (China)*	Timeless, enduring love
August 13 *Moria's Day (Rome)*	Improving one's fate in life or love
September 1 *Radha's Day (India)*	Celebrating joyful relationships

September 7 *Festival of Durga (Hindu)*	Love conquering all
October 18 *St. Luke's Day (England)*	Performing love divination
October 27 *Allen Apple Day (Cornwall)*	Working love magic or divination
October 31 *Halloween (Celtic)*	Love divination
November 10 *Celebration for the Goddess of Reason (France)*	Honing clear reasoning
November 25 *St. Catherine's Day (England/Europe)*	Praying for help with relationships, especially for older people who want companionship
November 30 *St. Andrew's Day (Scotland)*	Improving one's appearance
December 17 *Saturnalia (Rome)*	Unbridled passion
December 21 *Feast of St. Thomas (England)*	Eating specially prepared foods to receive dreams of future loves (specifically onions)
December 25 *Yule (Various)*	Performing love spells

Bibliography

Budapest, Z. *Grandmother of Time*. San Francisco, CA: Harper & Row, 1989.

Budge, E.A. Wallis. *Amulets & Superstitions*. Oxford, England: Oxford University Press, 1930.

Cooley, Arnold. *Handbook of the Toilet*. Philadelphia, PA: JB Lippencott, 1873.

Cristiani, R.S. *Treatise on Perfumery*. Philadelphia, PA: Henry Carey Baird & Co., 1877.

Cunningham, Scott. *Crystal, Gem, and Metal Magic*. St. Paul, MN: Llewellyn Publications, 1995.

Cunningham, Scott. *Magic of Incense, Oils & Brews*. St. Paul, MN: Llewellyn Publications, 1988.

Dolnick, Barrie. *Simple Spells for Love*. New York, NY: Harmony Books, 1994.

Farrar, Janet and Stewart. *The Witch's Goddess*. Custer, WA: Phoenix Publications, 1989.

Gonzalez-Wippler, Migene. *Amulets & Talismans*. St. Paul, MN: Llewellyn Publications, 1995.

Gordon, Stuart. *Encyclopedia of Myths & Legends*. London, England: Headline Books, 1993.

Guiley, Rosemary Ellen. *Moonscapes*. New York, NY: Prentice Hall, 1991.

Hall, Manly P. *Secret Teachings of All Ages*. Los Angeles, CA: Philosophical Research Society, 1977.

Hasnas, Rachelle. *Pocket Guide to Bach Flower Essences*. Freedom, CA: The Crossing Press, 1997.

Keville, Kathy. *Pocket Guide to Aromatherapy*. Freedom, CA: The Crossing Press, 1996.

Kieckhefer, Richard. *Magic in the Middle Ages*. Cambridge, England: Cambridge University Press, 1989.

Kunz, George Frederick. *The Curious Lore of Precious Stones*. New York, NY: Dover Publications, 1913.

Leach, Maria, editor. *Standard Dictionary of Folklore, Mythology, and Legend*. New York, NY: HarperCollins, 1972.

Lorie, Peter. *Superstitions*. New York, NY: Simon and Schuster, 1992.

Miller, Gustavus H. *Ten Thousand Dreams Interpreted*. New York, NY: M.A. Donohue & Co., 1931.

Mitford, Miranda Bruce. *Illustrated Book of Signs & Symbols*. New York, NY: DK Publishing, 1996.

Newall, Venetia. *Encyclopedia of Witchcraft & Magic*. New York, NY: Dial Press, 1978.

Opie, Iona and Tatem, Moria. *A Dictionary of Superstitions*. Oxford, England: Oxford University Press, 1990.

Paulsen, Kathryn. *Witch's Potions & Spells*. Mt. Vernon, NY: Peter Pauper Press, 1971.

Telesco, Patricia. *Spinning Spells, Weaving Wonders*. Freedom, CA: The Crossing Press, 1996.

Telesco, Patricia. *Victorian Grimoire*. St. Paul, MN: Llewellyn Publications, 1992.

Thompson, C.J.S. *The Hand of Destiny*. New York, NY: Bell Publishing Company, 1989.

Walker, Barbara. *The Woman's Dictionary of Symbols & Sacred Objects*. San Francisco, CA: Harper and Row, 1988.

Waring, Philippa. *The Dictionary of Omens & Superstitions*. Secaucus, NJ: Chartwell Books, 1978.

BOOKS BY THE CROSSING PRESS

MORE BOOKS BY PATRICIA TELESCO:

FutureTelling: *A Complete Guide to Divination*

This cross-cultural encyclopedia of divination practices gives over 250 entries, from simple signs and omens of traditional folk magic to complex rituals of oracular consultation.

$16.95 • Paper • ISBN 0-89594-872-9

The Language of Dreams

Patricia Telesco outlines a creative, interactive approach to understanding the dream symbols of our inner life. Interpretations of more than 800 dream symbols incorporate multi-cultural elements with psychological, religious, folk, and historical meanings.

$16.95 • Paper • ISBN 0-89594-836-2

Spinning Spells, Weaving Wonders: *Modern Magic for Everyday Life*

This essential book of over 300 spells tells how to work with simple, easy-to-find components and focus creative energy to meet daily challenges with awareness, confidence, and humor.

$14.95 • Paper • ISBN 0-89594-803-6

Wishing Well: *Empowering Your Hopes and Dreams*

Blending folklore, magic, and creative visualization, author Patricia Telesco explains how reclaiming the practice of Wishcraft can create our reality exactly as we wish it to be.

$14.95 • Paper • ISBN 0-89594-870-2

To receive a current catalog from The Crossing Press
please call toll-free, 800-777-1048.
Visit our Web site: www. crossingpress.com